COL

POCKET *School* THESAURUS

HarperCollins*Publishers*

First Published 1995

Reprinted 1995, 1997, 1998 (three times)

Latest reprint 1999

7 8 9

PO Box, Glasgow G4 0NB

The HarperCollins website address is
www.**fire**and**water**.com

ISBN 0 00 470784-2

A catalogue record for this book is available
from the British Library.

Corpus Acknowledgements
We would like to thank those authors and publishers
who kindly gave permission for copyright material to be
used in the Bank of English. We would also like to thank
Times Newspapers Ltd for providing valuable data.

Typeset by Morton Word Processing Ltd,
Scarborough, England

Printed and bound in Great Britain
by Caledonian International Book Manufacturing Ltd,
Glasgow G64

EDITORIAL STAFF

Managing Editor
Marian Makins

Senior Editor
Lorna Knight

Lexicographers
Ian Brookes
Mary O'Neill

Computing Staff
Jane Creevy

Introduction

Collins Pocket School Thesaurus has been specially written for school students in the 9-14 age range. The word "thesaurus" comes from a Greek word meaning "treasury" or "storehouse", and a thesaurus is a treasury or storehouse of words for you to draw on. It gives you lists of synonyms – words which mean the same, or almost the same, as the one you already have in mind, so that you can choose an alternative.

There are many reasons why you might want to look for a different word to use. Perhaps you want to avoid using the same word more than once, or perhaps the one that comes to mind first does not quite get across the exact meaning of what you want to say, or is too informal for the style in which you are writing.

The *Collins Pocket School Thesaurus* is arranged in a single alphabetical list of main-entry words, like a dictionary. To find exactly the right word for your purpose, look up the word which is your starting point. There, you will find a selection of alternatives which can be used to replace it. If the original word has more than one meaning, the alternative words are grouped in separate numbered lists. In addition, clear definitions of each word and each sense are given, so that the student can be confident of making the right choice. And to help the user even further, an example is given for each sense of each word, showing how it is used. These examples are taken from the Bank of English, an impressive database of over 200 million words of written and spoken English, so that they represent the words as they are really used.

The layout is very attractive and readable. All entry words are printed in colour, making it easy and quick to find the word you are looking for. And different senses are clearly numbered in colour, with all the synonyms also given in colour, so that you can find your way around the text very easily.

Not all words can be used in every situation. Some words are more suitable for spoken rather than written language, or are restricted in use to certain regions. These words are clearly marked to show their appropriate contexts, with labels like slang, informal, formal, British, French, U.S., and literary.

When you are choosing an alternative word from the list given, remember that the context is important. One word may be more appropriate as a substitute for the word you have in mind in one situation, while another is more suitable in a different context. The list of synonyms given for a main entry word or sense may cover several slightly different shades of meaning, so you must think carefully before choosing one as an alternative.

In addition to giving practical everyday help in all contexts and situations where good English is required, the thesaurus, especially when used in conjunction with its companion volume, the *Collins Pocket School Dictionary*, will help you to increase your vocabulary and develop your language skills.

GUIDE TO THE THESAURUS

Entry Word

critical

1. (adjective) A critical time is one which is very important in determining what happens in the future.

e.g. *a critical point in his career.*

crucial decisive momentous pivotal vital

Definition

2. A critical situation is a very serious one.

e.g. *The economy is in a critical state.*

dangerous grave perilous precarious serious

3. If you are critical of something or someone, you criticize them.

e.g. *His critical attitude puts a lot of people off.*

Synonyms

carping cavilling censorious derogatory disparaging scathing

criticize

Part of Speech

(verb) If you criticize someone or something, you say what you think is wrong with them.

e.g. *My parents criticized me endlessly.*

censure condemn disparage find fault with knock *informal* put down slag *informal* slate *informal*

Label

cross

1. (verb) If you cross something such as a room or a road, you go to the other side of it.

e.g. *He crossed over to the phone.*

bridge ford go across span traverse

Sense Number

2. Lines or roads that cross meet and go across each other.

e.g. *The pipe crossed under the road.*

crisscross intersect meet

3. (noun) Something that is a cross between two things is neither one thing nor the other, but a mixture of both.

Example

e.g. *a cross between a donkey and a horse.*

blend combination crossbreed hybrid mixture mongrel

A a

abandon

(verb) If you abandon someone or something, you leave them or give them up permanently.

e.g. *Carolyn abandoned her car.*

desert evacuate forsake jilt leave quit vacate

ability

(noun) Your ability to do something is the quality of intelligence or skill that you have that enables you to do it.

e.g. *the ability to get on with others.*

aptitude capability capacity competence expertise facility faculty flair gift knack power proficiency skill talent

able

1. (adjective) If you are able to do something, you can do it.

e.g. *I may be able to call you later.*

adequate capable fit

2. Someone who is able is very clever or talented.

e.g. *Charles is a very able journalist.*

accomplished adept capable clever competent efficient experienced expert gifted masterly practised proficient qualified skilful skilled talented

abnormality

(noun) An abnormality is something that is not normal or usual.

e.g. *an abnormality in the heart.*

aberration deviation eccentricity irregularity oddity peculiarity singularity

abolish

(verb) To abolish something means to put an end to it officially.

e.g. *a bill to abolish the death penalty.*

- annul axe cancel do away with eliminate end repeal revoke stamp out suppress wipe out

absent

(adjective) Something that is absent is not present in a place or situation.

e.g. *The ambassador planned to be absent from Moscow.*

away elsewhere gone lacking missing out wanting

absorb

(verb) If something absorbs liquid or gas, it soaks it up.

e.g. *Plants absorb carbon dioxide from the air.*

assimilate digest receive soak up take in

abstain

(verb) If you abstain from something, you do not do it or have it.

e.g. *The patients had to abstain from alcohol.*

avoid deny yourself forgo give up refrain from stop

absurd

(adjective) ridiculous and stupid.

e.g. *an absurd suggestion.*

crazy farcical foolish idiotic illogical irrational ludicrous nonsensical preposterous ridiculous senseless silly stupid

abundance

(noun) Something that exists in abundance exists in large numbers.

e.g. *an abundance of wildlife.*

bounty plenty profusion proliferation wealth

abuse

1. (noun) Abuse is cruel and violent treatment of someone.
e.g. *child abuse.*
damage harm hurt ill-treatment maltreatment misuse

2. (verb) If you abuse someone, you speak insultingly to them.
e.g. *a five-match ban for abusing the referee.*
curse insult libel malign slander smear vilify

3. To abuse someone also means to treat them cruelly and violently.
e.g. *parents suspected of abusing their children.*
damage hurt ill-treat injure maltreat misuse

abyss

(noun) An abyss is a very deep hole.
e.g. *She fell into a deep abyss.*
chasm gulf pit void

accidental

(adjective) happening by chance.
e.g. *accidental damage.*
casual chance fortuitous inadvertent unintentional unplanned unpremeditated

accommodation

(noun) Accommodation is a place provided for someone to sleep, work, or live in.
e.g. *They helped her to find accommodation and a job.*
board digs house housing lodgings quarters shelter

accomplice

(noun) An accomplice is a person who helps someone else to commit a crime.
e.g. *His accomplice was jailed for twelve months.*
accessory collaborator helper henchman partner

accurate

(adjective) completely true, correct, or precise.

e.g. *an accurate picture of events.*

correct exact faithful faultless meticulous precise right spot-on true truthful unerring

accustom

(verb) If you accustom yourself to something new or different, you get used to it.

e.g. *He tried to accustom himself to the darkness.*

acclimatize adapt condition familiarize habituate

achieve

(verb) If you achieve something, you successfully do it or cause it to happen.

e.g. *Dr Dalton has achieved some striking results.*

accomplish attain bring about carry out do effect fulfil get obtain perform reach realize win

acknowledge

(verb) If you acknowledge a fact or situation, you agree or admit that it is true.

e.g. *He did not like to acknowledge weakness.*

accept admit allow concede confess grant own recognize

acquit

(verb) If someone is acquitted of a crime, they have been tried in a court and found not guilty.

e.g. *She was acquitted of murder.*

absolve clear exonerate free

act

1. (verb) If you act in a play or film, you play a part.

e.g. *She had been acting in television sitcoms since she was a child.*

enact perform play portray represent

2. (noun) An act is a single thing that someone does.
e.g. *It was an act of disloyalty to the King.*
action deed exploit feat operation step stroke

3. An Act of Parliament is a law passed by the government.
e.g. *the Wildlife and Countryside Act.*
bill decree edict law legislation measure ordinance statute

acting

(adjective) Acting is used before the title of a job to show that someone is doing that job temporarily.
e.g. *the acting head of department.*
interim provisional substitute surrogate temporary

activate

(verb) To activate something means to cause it to start working.
e.g. *The driver activated his electronic window.*
actuate initiate set in motion set off start switch on trigger

actor

(noun) An actor is a man or woman whose profession is acting in plays, television, or films.
e.g. *My drama teacher said I should become an actor.*
actress performer player

addition

(noun) An addition is something that has been added to something else.
e.g. *Carrots are a welcome addition to a horse's diet.*
adjunct attachment extension extra supplement

adequate

(adjective) enough in amount or good enough for a purpose.
e.g. *an adequate diet.*
enough fair passable satisfactory sufficient

advance

(noun) Advance in something is progress in it.

e.g. *scientific advance.*

development progress step forward

advertise

(verb) If you advertise something, you tell people about it in a newspaper or poster, or on TV.

e.g. *Kasparov is paid a small fortune to advertise drinks.*

announce plug *slang* promote publicize push *informal*

advertisement

(noun) An advertisement is an announcement about something in a newspaper or poster, or on TV.

e.g. *an advertisement for a new magazine.*

ad *informal* advert *informal* announcement commercial notice plug *slang* promotion publicity

advice

(noun) Advice is an opinion or suggestion from someone about what you should do.

e.g. *He sought my advice as to how a chef should behave.*

counsel guidance help opinion recommendation suggestion view

advise

(verb) If you advise someone to do something, you tell them that you think they should do it.

e.g. *Steve's mother advised him to cancel his trip.*

counsel guide recommend suggest urge

affect

(verb) If something affects you, it influences you or changes you in some way.

e.g. *This experience affected her deeply.*

alter change concern influence

afraid

(adjective) If you are afraid, you are very frightened.
e.g. *I am afraid of flying.*
alarmed apprehensive fearful frightened nervous scared terrified

after

1. (preposition) later than a particular time, date, or event.
e.g. *I'll come round after dinner.*
following

2. (adverb) at a later time.
e.g. *Christopher was taken to hospital but died soon after.*
afterwards later subsequently thereafter

again

(adverb) returning to the same state or place as before.
e.g. *Her back began to hurt her again.*
afresh anew once more

aggressive

(adjective) full of anger, hostility, and violence.
e.g. *an aggressive crowd.*
antagonistic belligerent hostile pugnacious quarrelsome truculent

agonizing or agonising

(adjective) extremely painful, either physically or mentally.
e.g. *an agonizing decision.*
excruciating painful

agony

(noun) very great physical or mental pain.
e.g. *He crashed to the ground in agony.*
anguish distress hell misery pain suffering torment torture

agree

1. (verb) If you agree with someone, you have the same opinion as them.

e.g. *Plenty of experts agree with him.*

accord concur

2. If you agree to do something, you say that you will do it.

e.g. *I agreed to return to London.*

accede acquiesce assent comply consent

agreement

1. (noun) An agreement is a joint decision that has been reached by two or more people.

e.g. *I signed an agreement with the US Army.*

arrangement bargain compact contract covenant deal pact settlement treaty understanding

2. Two people who are in agreement have the same opinion about something.

e.g. *All were in agreement about the excellent performance.*

accord accordance concord concurrence harmony

aim

1. (verb) If you aim an object or weapon at someone or something, you point it at them.

e.g. *He aimed the gun at two pupils.*

direct level point

2. If you aim to do something, you are planning or hoping to do it.

e.g. *We aim to improve standards.*

aspire intend mean plan propose seek want wish

3. If you aim an action at a particular group, you intend them to be influenced by it.

e.g. *an anti-smoking campaign aimed at teenagers.*

direct level

4. (noun) Your aim is what you intend to achieve.

e.g. *My aim is to win a lot more races.*

ambition aspiration desire end goal intent intention object objective purpose target wish

alert

(adjective) paying full attention to what is happening.

e.g. *The criminal was spotted by an alert member of the public.*

attentive observant perceptive vigilant watchful wide-awake

alias

(noun) An alias is a false name used by a criminal.

e.g. *He had been operating under an alias.*

assumed name pseudonym

alive

(adjective) living.

e.g. *Both his parents are still alive.*

animate breathing live living

alliance

(noun) An alliance is a group of people, organizations, or countries working together for similar aims.

e.g. *a military alliance.*

affiliation association coalition confederation federation league union

all right

(adjective) If something is all right, it is satisfactory or acceptable.

e.g. *At first glance, everything looked all right.*

acceptable adequate fair fine not bad okay *informal*

ally

1. (noun) An ally is a person, organization, or country that helps and supports another.

e.g. *a close ally of the Labour leader.*

associate colleague confederate friend helper partner

2. (verb) If you ally yourself with someone, you agree to help and support each other.

e.g. *I won't ally myself with other childless women.*

affiliate associate

almost

(adverb) very nearly, but not completely or exactly.

e.g. *Over the past decade their wages have almost doubled.*

about all but nearly practically virtually

alone

1. (adjective) not with other people or things.

e.g. *He just wanted to be alone.*

apart isolated separate single single-handed solitary unaccompanied

2. (adverb) not with other people or things.

e.g. *She alone believed his story.*

only unaccompanied

aloud

(adverb) When you read or speak aloud, you speak loudly enough for other people to hear you.

e.g. *Our father read aloud to us after supper.*

audibly clearly distinctly out loud plainly

amaze

(verb) If something amazes you, it surprises you very much.

e.g. *We have been absolutely amazed by their friendliness.*

astonish astound bowl over daze dumbfound flabbergast stagger stun surprise

amazing

(adjective) very surprising, remarkable, or difficult to believe.

e.g. *an amazing story.*

fabulous incredible unbelievable wonderful

among or amongst

(preposition) surrounded by.
e.g. *The bike lay among piles of chains and pedals.*
amid amidst between with

amount

(noun) An amount of something is how much there is of it.
e.g. *a tiny amount of water.*
degree extent measure number quantity volume

ancestor

(noun) Your ancestors are the members of your family who lived many years ago and from whom you are descended.
e.g. *I'm rather proud of my Russian ancestors.*
forebear forefather predecessor progenitor

ancestry

(noun) Your ancestry consists of the people from whom you are descended.
e.g. *a French citizen of Greek ancestry.*
lineage pedigree stock

anger

1. (noun) Anger is the strong feeling that you get when you feel that someone has behaved in an unfair, cruel, or insulting way.
e.g. *The crowd went wild with anger.*
fury indignation ire outrage rage spleen temper wrath

2. (verb) If something angers you, it makes you feel angry.
e.g. *This attitude has angered his family.*
enrage incense infuriate madden outrage rile

angry

(adjective) very cross or annoyed.
e.g. *An angry crowd gathered on the steps.*

enraged furious incensed indignant infuriated irate livid outraged raging wrathful

animal

(noun) An animal is any living being except a plant, or any mammal except a human being.

e.g. *She kept most of the animals in small cages.*

beast brute creature

announce

(verb) If you announce something, you tell people about it publicly or officially.

e.g. *The team was announced on Friday morning.*

broadcast declare proclaim publish reveal tell

annoy

(verb) If someone or something annoys you, they irritate you and make you fairly angry.

e.g. *Elsie was annoyed by Ford's letter.*

aggravate exasperate gall harass hassle irk irritate needle nettle pester plague provoke rile vex

annul

(verb) If a marriage or contract is annulled, it is declared invalid, so that legally it is considered never to have existed.

e.g. *The marriage was annulled after a legal battle.*

cancel dissolve invalidate nullify repeal rescind revoke

answer

1. (verb) If you answer someone, you reply to them using words or actions or in writing.

e.g. *No one answered him.*

reply respond retort riposte

2. (noun) An answer is the reply you give when you answer someone.

e.g. *I knew the answer to that question.*

rejoinder reply response retort riposte

apathetic

(adjective) not interested in anything.

e.g. *Young people who have never had a job may become depressed and apathetic.*

half-hearted indifferent uninterested

apparent

(adjective) seeming real rather than actually being real.

e.g. *the apparent success of their marriage.*

ostensible outward seeming

appear

1. (verb) When something which you could not see appears, it moves (or you move) so that you can see it.

e.g. *Four or five dolphins suddenly appeared.*

come into view emerge materialize show

2. When something new appears, it begins to exist.

e.g. *The book first appeared three years ago.*

arise come into existence emerge occur turn up

appointment

(noun) An appointment is an arrangement you have with someone to meet or visit them.

e.g. *an appointment with a doctor.*

arrangement booking date engagement meeting rendezvous tryst

appreciate

(verb) If you appreciate something, you like it because you recognize its good qualities.

e.g. *He appreciates fine wines.*

esteem like prize regard respect value

approval

(noun) Approval is agreement given to a plan or request.

e.g. *The plan will require approval from the local authority.*

agreement assent authorization blessing consent endorsement okay permission sanction

approve

1. (verb) If you approve of something, you think that it is right or good.

e.g. *My mother doesn't approve of smoking.*

acclaim admire applaud commend esteem favour like praise respect

2. If someone in a position of authority approves a plan or idea, they formally agree to it.

e.g. *The board of ministers unanimously approved the project.*

accept allow authorize endorse pass permit ratify sanction

approximate

(adjective) almost accurate or exact.

e.g. *What was the approximate distance between the cars?*

close estimated near rough

area

(noun) An area is a particular part of a place, country, or the world.

e.g. *a built-up area of London.*

district locality neighbourhood part patch portion region section sector stretch vicinity zone

arrest

(verb) If the police arrest someone, they take them into custody to decide whether to charge them with an offence.

e.g. *We want the police to arrest the criminals.*

apprehend capture catch detain seize stop take

assess

(verb) If you assess something, you consider it carefully and make a judgment about it.

e.g. *The two of them assessed the challenge.*

appraise evaluate gauge judge size up

assign

1. (verb) To assign something to someone means to give it to them officially or to make them responsible for it.

e.g. *He was assigned a cabin in first class.*

allocate allot consign give grant

2. If someone is assigned to do something, they are officially told to do it.

e.g. *Fox had been assigned to do an article on the Lucan case.*

appoint choose name nominate select

associate

(verb) If you associate with a group of people, you spend a lot of time with them.

e.g. *He spent a lot of time associating with criminals.*

consort fraternize hobnob mix

assume

1. (verb) If you assume that something is true, you accept that it is true even though you have not thought about it.

e.g. *Patients often assumed I was a doctor.*

accept believe expect fancy imagine suppose surmise suspect think

2. To assume responsibility for something means to put yourself in charge of it.

e.g. *He assumed command of the navy.*

accept shoulder take on take over take up undertake

3. If you assume a particular appearance, you start to have it.

e.g. *He assumed an expression of indifference.*

adopt affect feign put on sham simulate

attack

1. (verb) To attack someone means to use violence against them so as to hurt or kill them.

e.g. *He was attacked by thugs with metal bats.*

assail assault set about set upon

2. (noun) An attack is violent physical action against someone.

e.g. *an appalling and unprovoked attack.*

assault offensive onslaught

3. (verb) If you attack someone or their ideas, you criticize them strongly.

e.g. *He attacked the government's economic policies.*

abuse blame censure criticize vilify

attractive

1. (adjective) interesting and possibly advantageous.

e.g. *an attractive proposition.*

agreeable appealing interesting inviting tempting

2. pleasant to look at or be with.

e.g. *an attractive woman.*

appealing beautiful captivating charming engaging fetching gorgeous handsome lovely pleasing pretty winsome

attribute

(verb) If you attribute something to a circumstance, person, or thing, you believe that it was caused or created by that circumstance, person, or thing.

e.g. *Water pollution was attributed to the use of fertilizers.*

ascribe blame charge impute

automatic

(adjective) An automatic machine is programmed to perform tasks without needing a person to operate it.

e.g. *The plane was flying on automatic pilot.*

mechanical mechanized

available

(adjective) Something that is available can be obtained.

e.g. *These products are available in health-food shops.*

accessible attainable obtainable

avant-garde

(adjective) extremely modern or experimental, especially in art, literature, or music.

e.g. *avant-garde jazz.*

experimental innovative innovatory pioneering progressive

average

(adjective) Average means standard, normal, or usual.

e.g. *the average American teenager.*

general normal ordinary regular standard typical usual

avoid

1. (verb) If you avoid doing something, you make a deliberate effort not to do it.

e.g. *It is wise to avoid eating fat.*

bypass circumvent dodge evade shirk side-step

2. If you avoid someone, you keep away from them.

e.g. *He tried to avoid his landlady whenever possible.*

dodge elude evade shun

aware

(adjective) If you are aware of something, you know about it or realize that it is there.

e.g. *We have to make people aware of the dangers.*

conscious knowing mindful

awful

(adjective) very unpleasant or very bad.

e.g. *He was an awful painter.*

appalling deplorable dire dreadful fearful frightful

ghastly hideous horrible nasty shocking terrible
unpleasant

awkward

1. (adjective) clumsy and uncomfortable.

e.g. *an awkward, stooping movement.*

clumsy graceless ham-fisted ham-handed
maladroit *formal* ungainly ungraceful

2. embarrassed, shy, or nervous.

e.g. *She may feel a little awkward with us all at first.*

discomfited embarrassed ill at ease nervous out of place
self-conscious shy

B b

backbone

1. (noun) A backbone is the column of linked bones along the middle of a person's or animal's back.

e.g. *Apply pressure on the middle of the backbone with your fist.*

spinal column spine vertebrae

2. Backbone is also strength of character.

e.g. *His trouble was lack of backbone.*

courage determination firmness fortitude grit mettle nerve pluck

backside

(noun; an informal word) Your backside is the part of your body that you sit on.

e.g. *She slipped and slid downhill on her backside.*

bottom posterior rear rump

bad

1. (adjective) evil or immoral in character or behaviour.

e.g. *a bad person.*

corrupt criminal delinquent evil immoral mean sinful vile villainous wicked

2. insufficient or of poor quality.

e.g. *The pay was bad.*

defective deficient faulty imperfect inadequate incorrect inferior poor unsatisfactory

3. Bad food is not suitable for eating, because it has started to decay.

e.g. *a bad egg.*

decayed mouldy off putrid rancid rotten sour substandard unhealthy

ball

(noun) A ball is any object shaped like a sphere, especially one used in games such as tennis, cricket, and football.

e.g. *A child threw a ball of newspaper into the road.*

globe orb pellet sphere

ban

1. (verb) If something is banned, or if you are banned from doing it or using it, you are not allowed to do it or use it.

e.g. *proposals to ban smoking.*

bar boycott debar forbid outlaw prohibit proscribe

2. (noun) If there is a ban on something, it is not allowed.

e.g. *a ban on fox hunting.*

embargo prohibition proscription restriction suppression

banish

(verb) To banish someone means to send them into exile.

e.g. *He was banished to Germany.*

deport exile expel outlaw transport

bare

1. (adjective) If a part of your body is bare, it is not covered by any clothing.

e.g. *bare legs.*

exposed naked nude stark stripped uncovered undressed

2. If something is bare, it has nothing on top of it or inside it.

e.g. *a small bare office.*

blank denuded empty poor scanty unfurnished vacant

barrage

1. (noun) A barrage of questions or complaints is a lot of them all coming at the same time.

e.g. *The news was greeted with a barrage of criticism.*

bombardment onslaught storm volley

2. A barrage is continuous artillery fire over a wide area, to prevent the enemy from moving.
e.g. *Police came under a barrage of missiles.*
battery bombardment fusillade salvo shelling volley

barren

1. (adjective) Barren land has soil of such poor quality that plants cannot grow on it.
e.g. *a barren, waterless desert.*
arid desolate dry empty infertile unproductive waste

2. If a female is barren, she is physically incapable of having offspring.
e.g. *a three-year-old barren mare.*
childless infertile sterile

barrier

(noun) A barrier is a fence or wall that prevents people or animals getting from one area to another.
e.g. *Jim had climbed over the barrier on to the track.*
bar barricade fence obstruction railing

base

1. (noun) The base of something is its lowest part, which often supports the rest.
e.g. *the base of the hill.*
bed bottom foot foundation pedestal rest stand support

2. (adjective; a literary use) A base act is one which is shocking and contemptible.
e.g. *He would never suspect her of so base a betrayal.*
contemptible despicable dishonourable ignoble low mean shameful

basic

(adjective) The basic aspects of something are the most necessary ones.

e.g. *the basic necessities of life.*
central elementary essential fundamental intrinsic key primary rudimentary underlying vital

basis

1. (noun) The basis of something is the essential main principle from which it can be developed.
e.g. *The same colour theme is used as the basis for several patterns.*
base foundation groundwork

2. The basis for a belief is the facts that support it.
e.g. *There is no basis for this assumption.*
foundation ground support

bay

(noun) A bay is a part of a coastline where the land curves inwards.
e.g. *We anchored one evening in a deserted bay.*
cove gulf inlet sound

beach

(noun) A beach is an area of sand or pebbles beside the sea.
e.g. *The beach stretches along the west coast.*
coast sands seashore seaside shore strand

beat

1. (verb) To beat someone or something means to hit them hard and repeatedly.
e.g. *He threatened to beat her.*
batter buffet flog hit lash pound punch strike thrash whip

2. If you beat someone in a race, game, or competition, you defeat them or do better than them.
e.g. *County beat Brighton 3-1 in the final.*
conquer defeat lick *informal* outdo overcome surpass trounce vanquish

beautiful

(adjective) very attractive or pleasing.

e.g. *beautiful harmonies.*

appealing charming comely delightful exquisite glamorous gorgeous handsome lovely ravishing stunning

before

(adverb) If you have done something before, you have done it on a previous occasion.

e.g. *Never before had I seen such a moon.*

beforehand earlier formerly previously sooner

beg

(verb) When people beg, they ask for food or money, because they are very poor.

e.g. *She was reduced to begging on the streets.*

beseech cadge entreat implore importune plead pray solicit

begin

(verb) If you begin to do something, you start doing it. When something begins, it starts.

e.g. *I began to walk back to the car.*

commence initiate instigate institute launch prepare set about start

beginner

(noun) A beginner is someone who has just started learning to do something and cannot do it very well yet.

e.g. *Smaller sails are easier for beginners to handle.*

amateur apprentice fledgling learner novice recruit tyro

belief

(noun) A belief is one of the principles of a religion or moral system.

e.g. *their belief in equality.*

creed doctrine ideology philosophy principles tenet

belittle

(verb) If you belittle someone or something, you make them seem unimportant.

e.g. *He derided my taste and belittled my opinions.*

decry denigrate diminish disparage

beloved

(adjective) A beloved person or thing is one that you feel a great affection for.

e.g. *Someone stole my beloved bicycle.*

adored cherished darling dear dearest loved precious sweet

bench

(noun) A bench is a long seat that two or more people can sit on.

e.g. *We sat on a concrete bench in the sun.*

form pew seat

bend

1. (verb) When you bend something, you use force to make it curved or angular.

e.g. *Most magicians can bend spoons or keys.*

buckle crook curve flex twist warp

2. When you bend, you move your head and shoulders forwards and downwards.

e.g. *He bent to untie his shoes.*

lean stoop

benefactor

(noun) A benefactor is a person who helps to support a person or institution by giving money.

e.g. *An anonymous benefactor stepped in to provide the prize money.*

backer patron promoter sponsor

beneficial

(adjective) Something that is beneficial is good for people.

e.g. *the beneficial effects of exercise.*

advantageous favourable helpful profitable useful valuable wholesome

benefit

1. (noun) The benefits of something are the advantages that it brings to people.

e.g. *the benefits of relaxation.*

advantage asset blessing boon gain good help profit

2. (verb) If you benefit from something, or if something benefits you, it helps you.

e.g. *The children benefit from having regular playmates.*

aid assist gain profit

beside

(preposition) If one thing is beside something else, they are next to each other.

e.g. *a house beside the sea.*

adjacent to alongside near neighbouring next to overlooking

best

(adjective) superior to everything else of its type.

e.g. *the best holiday I ever had.*

choice elite finest first first-rate foremost leading outstanding perfect pre-eminent superlative supreme top

betray

1. (verb) If you betray someone who trusts you, you do something which harms them, such as helping their enemies.

e.g. *This individual was willing to betray his master.*

abandon desert double-cross forsake give away sell out

2. If you betray a secret, you tell it to someone you should not tell it to.

e.g. *He was jailed for betraying top-secret information.*
disclose divulge give away tell

3. If you betray your feelings or thoughts, you show them without intending to.
e.g. *His face betrayed nerves.*
evince expose give away reveal show

better

(adjective) superior to others.
e.g. *much better than expected.*
excelling finer fitter greater preferable superior surpassing worthier

beware

(verb) If you tell someone to beware of something, you are warning them that it might be dangerous or harmful.
e.g. *Police have warned the public to beware of an escaped prisoner.*
be careful look out mind shun watch out

bias

(noun) Someone who shows bias unfairly favours one person or thing.
e.g. *Tests have to be carefully constructed in order to avoid bias.*
bigotry discrimination favouritism leaning partiality prejudice slant

biased

(adjective) favouring one person or thing unfairly.
e.g. *biased attitudes.*
bigoted one-sided partial partisan predisposed prejudiced slanted weighted

big

(adjective) large in size, extent, or importance.
e.g. *a big house.*
bulky considerable eminent extensive important large

prodigious prominent serious significant sizeable spacious substantial

bill

(noun) A bill is a written statement of how much is owed for goods or services.

e.g. *We received a telephone bill for forty-four pounds.*

account charges invoice reckoning

bit

(noun) A bit of something is a small amount of it.

e.g. *a bit of coal.*

crumb fragment grain iota jot mite morsel part piece scrap

bitter

1. (adjective) If someone is bitter, they feel angry and resentful.

e.g. *a bitter and hateful old man.*

acrimonious embittered resentful sore sour

2. In a bitter argument or war, people argue or fight fiercely and angrily.

e.g. *a bitter power struggle.*

acrimonious hostile rancorous

3. Something that tastes bitter has a sharp, unpleasant taste.

e.g. *The coffee was bitter.*

acid acrid astringent sharp sour tart vinegary

black

(adjective) A surface that is completely black reflects no light at all.

e.g. *the black night air.*

dark dusky ebony jet pitch-black sable

blame

1. (verb) If someone blames you for something bad that has happened, they believe you caused it or are responsible for it.

e.g. *My father does not blame you for what Arthur did.*
accuse charge hold responsible reproach

2. (noun) The blame for something bad is the responsibility for causing it.
e.g. *He had to take the blame for everything.*
culpability fault guilt liability onus responsibility

blank

(adjective) If you look blank, your face shows no feeling, understanding, or interest.
e.g. *blank stares.*
expressionless impassive uncomprehending vacant vacuous

blasphemy

(noun) Blasphemy is speech or behaviour that shows disrespect for God or for things people regard as holy.
e.g. *a radio play full of shrieks, obscenities and blasphemies.*
desecration impiety profanity sacrilege

bless

(verb) When a priest blesses people or things, he asks for God's favour and protection for them.
e.g. *The hospital chaplain said prayers and blessed the ward.*
consecrate dedicate sanctify

blessing

(noun) A blessing is something good that you are thankful for.
e.g. *Good health is the greatest blessing.*
advantage benefit boon bounty favour gift godsend

block

1. (noun) A block of something is a large rectangular piece of it.
e.g. *a block of marble.*
bar brick cake chunk cube hunk square

2. (verb) To block a road, channel, or pipe means to put

something across it so that nothing can get through.
e.g. *The vehicle was blocking a narrow country lane.*
choke clog close obstruct

3. If something blocks your view, it is in the way and prevents you from seeing what you want to see.
e.g. *TV cameras had blocked their view of the show.*
obstruct

4. If someone blocks something, they prevent it from happening.
e.g. *The council blocked his plans.*
check deter halt hinder impede obstruct stop

blockage

(noun) When there is a blockage in a pipe, tube, or tunnel, something is clogging it.
e.g. *Our workmen have cleared the blockage and the system is working.*
impediment obstruction stoppage

blunt

(adjective) If you are blunt, you say exactly what you think, without trying to be polite.
e.g. *He is blunt, outspoken, practical, and down to earth.*
abrupt bluff brusque forthright frank outspoken tactless

blush

(verb) If you blush, your face becomes redder than usual, because you are ashamed or embarrassed.
e.g. *Even to think about it made her blush with shame.*
colour crimson flush redden

board

(noun) Board is the meals provided when you stay somewhere.
e.g. *The price includes full board.*
food meals provisions

boast

(verb) If you boast about your possessions or achievements, you talk about them proudly, especially to impress other people.

e.g. *I boasted about my holiday in Thailand.*

blow your own trumpet brag crow exaggerate show off strut swagger

body

(noun) Your body is either all your physical parts or just your trunk, excluding your head and limbs.

e.g. *Her body felt stiff and painful.*

build figure form frame physique shape torso trunk

bog

(noun) A bog is an area of land which is wet and permanently spongy.

e.g. *Both waded into the four feet deep bog.*

fen marsh mire morass quagmire swamp

boil

(noun) A boil is a red swelling on your skin.

e.g. *Painful boils appeared on my face.*

carbuncle pustule

boisterous

(adjective) Someone who is boisterous is noisy, lively, and rather rough.

e.g. *They were a boisterous friendly couple.*

bouncy noisy riotous rollicking rowdy unruly wild

bold

1. (adjective) confident and not shy or embarrassed.

e.g. *He was not bold enough to ask them.*

audacious brash brazen dauntless enterprising fearless forward intrepid pert spirited

2. clear and noticeable.

e.g. *bold colours.*
bright colourful conspicuous eye-catching flashy lively loud prominent striking strong vivid

bomb

(verb) When a place is bombed, it is attacked with bombs.
e.g. *Threats were made to bomb his house.*
blast blitz blow up bombard destroy shell

bond

1. (noun) A bond is a close relationship between people.
e.g. *Females have a wonderful bond with their babies.*
affinity attachment connection link tie

2. Bonds are also feelings or obligations that force you to behave in a particular way.
e.g. *the social bonds of community.*
fetter tie

boring

(adjective) dull and uninteresting.
e.g. *I found staying at home rather boring.*
dull flat humdrum insipid monotonous routine tedious tiresome tiring wearisome

bossy

(adjective) A bossy person enjoys telling other people what to do.
e.g. *She remembers being a rather bossy little girl.*
dictatorial domineering high-handed imperious lordly overbearing tyrannical

botch

(verb; an informal word) If you botch something, you do it badly or clumsily.
e.g. *She had completely botched one of the tasks.*
bungle mess up mismanage screw up *informal* spoil

bounce

(verb) When an object bounces, it springs back from something after hitting it. If you bounce an object, such as a ball, you throw it against a surface to make it do this.

e.g. *A wheel flew off the car and bounced over the safety barrier.*

bound rebound recoil ricochet spring

boy

(noun) A boy is a male child.

e.g. *She gave birth to a healthy baby boy.*

lad stripling youngster youth

boycott

(verb) If you boycott a person, organization, product, or event, you refuse to have anything to do with it.

e.g. *The opposition is threatening to boycott parliament.*

black blacklist ostracize outlaw proscribe

brave

(adjective) A brave person is willing to do dangerous things and does not show any fear.

e.g. *an awards ceremony for brave firemen.*

bold courageous daring fearless gallant heroic intrepid plucky valiant

breach

(noun) A breach of an agreement or law is an action that breaks it.

e.g. *a breach of contract.*

contravention infringement transgression violation

break

1. (verb) When an object breaks, it is damaged and separates into pieces.

e.g. *A pane of glass broke in the kitchen.*

burst crack fracture fragment rupture shatter smash

snap splinter split tear

2. If you break a rule, promise, or agreement, you fail to keep it.
e.g. *Her employers were breaking the law.*
breach contravene disregard infringe transgress violate

breed

1. (verb) When animals breed, they mate and produce offspring.
e.g. *These birds usually attempt to breed during May to September.*
multiply procreate reproduce

2. (noun) A breed of animal is a particular type of it.
e.g. *I like most breeds of dogs.*
kind sort species stock strain type variety

brief

(adjective) Something that is brief lasts only a short time.
e.g. *They allowed him a brief rest.*
cursory fleeting limited little momentary quick short short-lived swift transitory

bright

(adjective) strong and startling.
e.g. *a bright light.*
blazing bold brilliant dazzling gleaming glistening glittering glowing intense luminous radiant vivid

broad-minded

(adjective) Someone who is broad-minded is tolerant of behaviour that other people may find upsetting or immoral.
e.g. *He knew his uncle to be a broad-minded man.*
indulgent liberal open-minded permissive tolerant

broke

(adjective; an informal use) If you are broke, you have no money.
e.g. *The company was broke.*

bankrupt insolvent penniless

bug

(noun; an informal use) A bug is a virus or minor infection.
e.g. *He was recovering from a stomach bug.*
disease germ infection microorganism virus

build

(verb) To build something such as a house or a bridge means to make it from its parts.
e.g. *The council decided to build a new civic centre.*
assemble construct erect fabricate form make put up raise

bulky

(adjective) large and heavy.
e.g. *a bulky package.*
cumbersome unmanageable unwieldy

bump

(noun) A bump on a surface is a raised, uneven part.
e.g. *The plane hit a bump on the runway.*
bulge hump lump protuberance swelling

burden

1. (noun) A burden is a heavy load.
e.g. *They carried the heavy burden to the gate.*
encumbrance load weight

2. If something is a burden to you, it causes you a lot of worry or hard work.
e.g. *My shyness was a terrible burden.*
affliction anxiety encumbrance millstone onus strain stress trial trouble weight worry

bureaucracy

(noun) Bureaucracy is the complex system of rules and routine

procedures which operate in government departments.
e.g. *I dislike excessive bureaucracy.*
officialdom red tape

burly

(adjective) A burly man has a broad body and strong muscles.
e.g. *burly security guards.*
beefy big brawny bulky hefty muscular powerful stocky strapping strong sturdy

burn

1. (verb) If something is burning, it is on fire.
e.g. *In her hut there was a candle burning.*
blaze flame flicker glow

2. To burn something means to destroy it with fire.
e.g. *He burned the documents and books.*
char ignite incinerate

burst

(noun) A burst of something is a short period of it.
e.g. *He had a sudden burst of energy.*
bout fit outbreak spate spell spurt

business

(noun) A business is an organization which produces or sells goods or provides a service.
e.g. *a small travel business.*
company concern enterprise firm industry organization venture

bustle

(noun) Bustle is busy, noisy activity.
e.g. *the perpetual bustle of the harbour.*
activity commotion excitement flurry fuss hurly-burly hurry rush stir to-do tumult

busy

(adjective) If you are busy, you are in the middle of doing something.

e.g. *George was busy preparing lunch.*

employed engaged engrossed occupied slaving working

buzz

(noun) A buzz is the sound something makes when it buzzes.

e.g. *a gentle buzz of conversation.*

drone hum

C c

call

1. (verb) If someone or something is called by a particular name, that is their name.

e.g. *a man called Jeffrey.*

christen designate dub entitle label name term

2. If someone is called before a court of law, they are ordered to appear there.

e.g. *She was called as a witness in the case.*

invite summon

calling

(noun) If you have a calling to a particular job, you have a strong feeling that you should do it.

e.g. *Saint Francis received his calling to repair God's church.*

mission vocation

callous

(adjective) cruel and showing no concern for other people's feelings.

e.g. *a callous criminal.*

cold hardened hardhearted heartless uncaring unfeeling

calm

1. (adjective) Someone who is calm is quiet and does not show any worry or excitement.

e.g. *I am very calm and rarely lose my temper.*

collected composed cool imperturbable placid quiet relaxed sedate self-possessed serene tranquil unflappable unruffled

2. (noun) Calm is a state of quietness and peacefulness.

e.g. *He liked the calm of the evening.*

calmness composure peacefulness serenity stillness tranquillity

3. (verb) To calm someone means to make them less upset or excited.

e.g. *She calmed us all down by reading aloud.*

allay hush lull mollify placate quieten relax soothe

campaign

(noun) A campaign is a planned set of actions aimed at achieving a particular result.

e.g. *a campaign to educate people.*

crusade drive movement push

cancer

(noun) Cancer is a serious disease in which abnormal cells in a part of the body increase rapidly, producing growths.

e.g. *stomach cancer.*

carcinoma tumour

capitalism

(noun) Capitalism is an economic and political system where business and industry are owned by private individuals and not by the state.

e.g. *the West's efforts to transform Russia from communism to capitalism.*

free enterprise private enterprise

captain

(noun) The captain of a ship is the officer in charge of it, especially a naval officer.

e.g. *the First Officer, the second ranking officer after the ship's captain.*

boss chief commander head leader master officer skipper

care

(verb) If you care for someone, you look after them.
e.g. *Children have to be cared for.*
look after   nurse   take care of   tend

careful

(adjective) acting sensibly and with care.
e.g. *Be careful what you say to him.*
cautious   chary   circumspect   mindful   particular   prudent   vigilant   wary   watchful

careless

(adjective) doing something badly without enough attention.
e.g. *careless driving.*
cavalier   haphazard   incautious   lackadaisical   lax   neglectful   negligent   offhand   perfunctory   slapdash   slipshod   sloppy *informal*   thoughtless   unthinking

caress

(verb) If you caress someone, you stroke them gently and affectionately.
e.g. *He caressed her hand.*
fondle   stroke

cargo

(noun) Cargo is the goods carried on a ship or plane.
e.g. *The planes will be used for cargo rather than passenger flights.*
consignment   freight   load   shipment

carry

(verb) When a vehicle carries people, they travel in it.
e.g. *The aircraft can carry as many as 39 passengers.*
bear   convey   take   transport

carve

(verb) To carve an object means to cut it out of a substance such as stone or wood.

e.g. *ancient Christian dwellings carved from stone.*

chisel cut engrave hew sculpt whittle

case

(noun) A case is a particular situation, event, or example.

e.g. *a clear case of mistaken identity.*

circumstance condition event example illustration instance occasion occurrence position situation specimen state

cast

(noun) The cast of a play or film is all the people who act in it.

e.g. *a largely unknown cast.*

actors characters company dramatis personae

casual

(adjective) careless or without interest.

e.g. *a casual glance over his shoulder.*

blasé indifferent nonchalant offhand perfunctory unconcerned

catch

1. (verb) To catch an animal means to stop it from moving freely after chasing or trapping it.

e.g. *He caught three fish in his net.*

bag capture ensnare entrap snare trap

2. When the police catch criminals, they find them and arrest them.

e.g. *Many offenders are not caught.*

apprehend arrest capture lift *slang* nail *informal* seize take prisoner

3. If you catch a cold or a disease, you become infected with it.

e.g. *I've caught that stomach bug that's going round.*

contract develop go down with

4. (noun) If there is a catch in something, there is a problem or hidden complication.

e.g. *When I said I'd do it, I didn't realise there was a catch.*

disadvantage drawback snag trap trick

cause

(verb) To cause something means to make it happen.

e.g. *A broken-down lorry is causing a tailback on the motorway.*

bring about create effect engender generate give rise to lead to occasion precipitate produce

celebrate

(verb) If you celebrate, or celebrate something, you do something special and enjoyable in honour of it.

e.g. *a party to celebrate the end of the exams.*

exult honour rejoice

censor

(verb) If someone censors a book or film, they cut or ban parts of it that are considered unsuitable for the public.

e.g. *Some argue that nothing should be censored, however unpleasant.*

bowdlerize cut expurgate

centralize

(verb) To centralize a system means to bring the organization of it under the control of one central group.

e.g. *a system for centralized record keeping.*

amalgamate concentrate incorporate rationalize streamline unify

centre

(noun) The centre of an object or area is the middle of it.

e.g. *a hotel in the centre of town.*

core heart hub middle

ceremony

(noun) A ceremony is a set of formal actions performed at a special occasion or important public event.

e.g. *his recent coronation ceremony.*

ceremonial rite ritual service

challenge

(verb) If you challenge something, you question whether it is correct or true.

e.g. *Local community groups challenged this argument.*

contradict defy dispute question

chance

(noun) Chance is the way things happen unexpectedly without being planned.

e.g. *I only found out by chance.*

accident coincidence destiny fate fluke fortune luck providence

change

1. (noun) A change in something is a difference or alteration.

e.g. *Steven soon noticed a change in Penny's attitude.*

adjustment alteration conversion difference metamorphosis modification transformation

2. (verb) When something changes or when you change it, it becomes different.

e.g. *My ideas have changed since then.*

adjust alter convert metamorphose modify transform

changeable

(adjective) likely to change all the time.

e.g. *changeable weather.*

capricious erratic fickle inconsistent mercurial temperamental unpredictable unstable variable volatile

character

(noun) The character of a person or place is all the qualities which combine to form their personality or atmosphere.

e.g. *His actions are typical of his brave and strong character.*

constitution disposition identity make-up nature personality quality temper temperament type

characteristic

1. (noun) A characteristic is a quality that is typical of a particular person or thing.

e.g. *Silence is the characteristic of the place.*

attribute feature mark peculiarity property quality trait

2. (adjective) Characteristic means typical of a particular person or thing.

e.g. *Two things are very characteristic of his driving.*

distinctive distinguishing idiosyncratic individual peculiar representative special specific typical

charm

(verb) If you charm someone, you use your ability to be attractive and pleasing on them.

e.g. *She charmed audiences as a comic opera singer.*

attract beguile bewitch captivate delight enchant entrance fascinate please

chase

(verb) If you chase someone or something, you run or go after them in order to catch them or drive them away.

e.g. *a group of children chasing a football.*

follow pursue run after

chat

1. (noun) A chat is a friendly talk with someone, usually about things that are not very important.

e.g. *He invited me into his living room for an informal chat.*

chatter gossip natter talk tête-à-tête

2. (verb) When people chat, they talk to each other in a friendly way.

e.g. *They were able to chat in more than one language.*

chatter gossip natter talk

cheap

(adjective) Something that is cheap costs very little money, and is sometimes of poor quality.

e.g. *a cheap hotel room.*

bargain cut-price economical inexpensive low-cost low-priced reasonable

cheat

(verb) If someone cheats, they do wrong or unfair things in order to win or get something that they want.

e.g. *We caught him cheating on an exam paper.*

con *informal* deceive defraud double-cross hoodwink swindle

cheek

(noun) Cheek is speech or behaviour that is rude or disrespectful.

e.g. *He had the cheek to say I should lose some weight.*

disrespect effrontery gall impertinence impudence insolence nerve temerity

cheer

(verb) If something cheers you, it makes you feel happier.

e.g. *I was cheered by the prospect of being able to help myself.*

brighten buoy up cheer up comfort console gladden hearten uplift

cheerful

(adjective) happy and in good spirits.

e.g. *I had never seen her so cheerful.*

blithe breezy bright buoyant cheery chirpy gay happy

hearty jaunty jocular jolly jovial joyful light-hearted merry sunny

cherish

1. (verb) If you cherish something, you care deeply about it and want to keep it or look after it lovingly.

e.g. *The previous owners had loved and cherished the house.*

care for treasure

2. If you cherish a memory or hope, you have it in your mind and care deeply about it.

e.g. *I cherish the good memories I have of him.*

cultivate entertain foster harbour hold dear nurse nurture sustain treasure

child

1. (noun) A child is a young person who is not yet an adult.

e.g. *She seemed no more than a child to him.*

baby infant juvenile kid *informal* minor nipper *informal* toddler tot youngster

2. Someone's child is their son or daughter.

e.g. *She took good care of her child.*

descendant issue offspring progeny

childish

(adjective) immature and foolish.

e.g. *I don't have time for childish arguments.*

babyish immature infantile juvenile puerile

choice

1. (noun) A choice is a range of different things that are available to choose from.

e.g. *a wider choice of treatments.*

alternative option selection variety

2. (adjective) Choice means of very high quality.

e.g. *choice food and drink.*

best elite excellent hand-picked prize select special

choose

(verb) To choose something means to decide to have it or do it.
e.g. *He chose to live in England.*
elect opt for pick select take

chop

(verb) To chop something means to cut it with quick, heavy strokes using an axe or a knife.
e.g. *Eric was in the kitchen chopping onions.*
hack hew lop

chronological

(adjective) arranged in the order in which things happened.
e.g. *Tell me the whole story in chronological order.*
consecutive historical

chunk

(noun) A chunk of something solid is a thick piece of it.
e.g. *a chunk of ice.*
block hunk lump mass piece portion slab wad

circulate

(verb) When you circulate something among people, you pass it round or tell it to all the people.
e.g. *We circulate a regular newsletter.*
broadcast disseminate distribute issue make known promulgate spread

city

(noun) A city is a large town where many people live and work.
e.g. *the shops and markets of the city.*
conurbation metropolis town

claim

(verb) If you claim that something is true or is the case, you say that it is, although some people may not believe you.

e.g. *He claims to have lived in the same house all his life.*

allege assert hold insist maintain profess uphold

class

(noun) A class of people or things is a group of them of a particular type or quality.

e.g. *the old class of politicians.*

category group kind order set sort type

clear

(adjective) easy to understand, see, or hear.

e.g. *He made it clear he did not want to talk.*

apparent certain coherent definite distinct evident explicit lucid manifest obvious patent plain positive pronounced unambiguous unequivocal

clever

(adjective) intelligent and quick to understand things.

e.g. *He was a very clever fellow with a research career.*

astute brainy *informal* bright brilliant intelligent quick sensible shrewd smart

climb

(verb) To climb means to move upwards.

e.g. *She climbed the stairs.*

ascend mount rise scale

clique

(noun) A clique is a small group of people who stick together and do not mix with other people.

e.g. *I don't have a little clique of friends.*

circle coterie crowd faction gang group set

close

(verb) If you close a meeting, conversation, or event, you bring it to an end.

e.g. *the men's road race, which closed the cycling programme.*

complete conclude end finish terminate wind up

cloth

(noun) Cloth is fabric made by a process such as weaving.

e.g. *the blue cloth of her jeans.*

fabric material textiles

clothe

(verb) To clothe someone means to give them clothes to wear.

e.g. *Relations used to tell my mother how to clothe me.*

attire dress garb

clothes

(plural noun) Clothes are the things people wear on their bodies.

e.g. *She wears very smart clothes.*

apparel attire clothing dress garb garments gear *informal* outfit togs *informal*

cloudy

(adjective) full of clouds.

e.g. *the cloudy sky.*

dark dim dismal dull gloomy leaden overcast

clown

(noun) You can refer to any funny or silly person as a clown.

e.g. *I can be a clown to make someone feel better.*

buffoon comedian fool jester joker

club

1. (noun) A club is an organization of people with a particular interest, who meet regularly; also the place where they meet.

e.g. *a science club.*
association company fraternity group guild league society

2. A club is also a thick, heavy stick used as a weapon.
e.g. *They beat him with a club.*
bat bludgeon cosh *British* cudgel stick truncheon

clumsy

1. (adjective) moving awkwardly and carelessly.
e.g. *He's so clumsy he's forever breaking things.*
awkward blundering bungling gawky heavy inept lumbering maladroit uncoordinated ungainly

2. said or done without thought or tact.
e.g. *his clumsy attempts to catch her out.*
awkward blundering bungling gauche inept maladroit

coach

1. (verb) If someone coaches you, they teach you and help you to get better at a sport or a subject.
e.g. *Laura had coached Jane in economics.*
drill instruct prepare teach train tutor

2. (noun) Someone's coach is a person who coaches them in a sport or a subject.
e.g. *my tennis coach.*
instructor teacher trainer tutor

coax

(verb) If you coax someone to do something, you gently persuade them to do it.
e.g. *We had a hard job coaxing her to come.*
cajole entice persuade talk into wheedle

collapse

(verb) If something such as a building collapses, it falls down suddenly. If a person collapses, they fall down suddenly because they are ill.

e.g. *He collapsed with exhaustion.*
break down faint fall fall down give way subside

colleague

(noun) A person's colleagues are the people he or she works with.
e.g. *Your colleagues will be concerned about your going to hospital.*
associate workmate

collection

(noun) A collection of things is a group of them acquired over a period of time.
e.g. *a collection of paintings.*
accumulation anthology compilation group set

collision

(noun) A collision occurs when a moving object hits something.
e.g. *a collision between two boats.*
accident bump crash impact pile-up smash

colloquial

(adjective) Colloquial words and phrases are informal and used especially in conversation.
e.g. *colloquial Scots.*
conversational idiomatic informal vernacular

colony

(noun) A colony is a country controlled by a more powerful country.
e.g. *Sri Lanka, a former British colony.*
outpost province settlement

colour

(noun) The colour of something is the appearance that it has as a result of reflecting light.
e.g. *ribbons of different colours.*
hue shade tint

come

(verb) If a feeling or situation comes from doing something, it is the result of it.

e.g. *the strength that comes from belonging to a family.*

arise emanate emerge happen issue occur originate result

come across

(verb) If you come across something, you find it by chance.

e.g. *I came across this old photo while I was clearing out a cupboard.*

chance on discover find stumble on

comedian

(noun) A comedian is an entertainer whose job is to make people laugh, especially by telling jokes or funny stories.

e.g. *the funniest comedian you've ever seen.*

clown comic entertainer humorist jester wit

comfortable

1. (adjective) Something that is comfortable makes you feel relaxed.

e.g. *The kitchen was a homely, comfortable room.*

cosy easy homely pleasant relaxing snug

2. You can say that someone is comfortable when they have enough money to live without financial problems.

e.g. *a plan for a comfortable retirement.*

affluent prosperous rich well-off well-to-do

command

(verb) To command someone to do something means to order them to do it.

e.g. *He commanded his troops to attack.*

bid charge direct enjoin order

commandeer

(verb) If soldiers commandeer something, they officially take it so that they can use it.

e.g. *The loads were commandeered by US troops.*

appropriate expropriate requisition seize

commemorate

(verb) If you commemorate an event, you do something special to show that you remember it.

e.g. *an exhibition to commemorate the 250th anniversary of the President's birth.*

celebrate honour keep remember

comment

(verb) If you comment on something, you make a remark about it.

e.g. *a plan of the essay for my tutor to comment on.*

mention note observe remark say

commit

(verb) To commit a crime or sin means to do it.

e.g. *a woman unlikely to commit murder.*

carry out do execute perform perpetrate

common

1. (adjective) If something is common knowledge or a common belief, it is widely known or believed.

e.g. *It is common knowledge that swimming is one of the best forms of exercise.*

accepted general popular prevailing prevalent universal widespread

2. If you describe someone as common, you mean they do not have good taste or good manners.

e.g. *The visitors were common and vulgar.*

coarse low plebeian vulgar

common sense

(noun) Your common sense is your natural ability to behave sensibly and make good judgments.

e.g. *He exhibits common sense in many of his views.*

good sense practicality prudence soundness wit

communicate

(verb) If you communicate an idea or a feeling to someone, you make them aware of it.

e.g. *The patient is unable to communicate his wishes.*

convey impart pass on transmit

company

(noun) If you have company, you have a friend or visitor with you.

e.g. *I enjoyed her company.*

companionship fellowship society

comparable

(adjective) If two things are comparable, they are similar in size or quality.

e.g. *He replaced the TV he'd broken with one of comparable value.*

alike commensurate corresponding equal equivalent on a par similar

compatible

(adjective) If people or things are compatible, they can live, exist, or work together successfully.

e.g. *We like each other and are compatible.*

harmonious suited well-matched

compensate

1. (verb) To compensate someone means to give them money to replace something lost, damaged, or destroyed.

e.g. *The cash will be used to compensate accident victims.*

recompense refund reimburse remunerate

2. If one thing compensates for another, it cancels out its bad effects.

e.g. *The trip more than compensated for the hardship.*

atone balance cancel (out) counteract make up for offset redress

complacent

(adjective) If someone is complacent, they are self-satisfied and unconcerned about a serious situation.

e.g. *We must never be complacent and say we're doing well enough.*

pleased with yourself self-satisfied smug

complain

(verb) If you complain, you say that you are not satisfied with something.

e.g. *She was always complaining about one thing or another.*

carp grizzle grouch *informal* grouse grumble lament moan whine whinge *informal*

complete

1. (adjective) to the greatest degree possible.

e.g. *He always makes a complete mess of things.*

absolute consummate outright perfect thorough total utter

2. If something is complete, none of it is missing.

e.g. *a complete set of tools.*

entire full intact perfect unbroken undivided whole

complex

(adjective) Something that is complex has many different parts and is complicated.

e.g. *a very complex problem.*

circuitous complicated convoluted intricate involved tangled tortuous

compulsory

(adjective) If something is compulsory, you have to do it.

e.g. *compulsory redundancies.*

binding forced mandatory obligatory

conceit

(noun) Conceit is someone's excessive pride in their appearance, abilities, or achievements.

e.g. *Self-confidence is not the same as conceit.*

arrogance bigheadedness *informal* egotism narcissism pride vanity

conceited

(adjective) Someone who is conceited is too proud of their appearance, abilities, or achievements.

e.g. *A conceited person boasts about her own achievements.*

arrogant big-headed egotistical narcissistic proud vain

concern

(verb) If something concerns you, it is important to you.

e.g. *Your personal problems don't concern me.*

affect be relevant to interest involve pertain to relate to

concise

(adjective) giving all the necessary information using the minimum number of words.

e.g. *a concise guide to each area.*

brief compact condensed laconic pithy short succinct

condemn

1. (verb) If you condemn something, you say it is bad and unacceptable.

e.g. *The ministers condemned the continued fighting.*

censure criticize damn denounce

2. If someone is condemned to a punishment, they are given it.

e.g. *The murderer was condemned to death.*

sentence

3. If you are condemned to something unpleasant, you must suffer it.

e.g. *many women who are condemned to poverty.*

doom sentence

condescending

(adjective) If you are condescending, you show by your behaviour that you think you are superior to other people.

e.g. *condescending sneers.*

disdainful lofty patronizing snobbish snooty supercilious superior

condition

(noun) A condition is a requirement that must be fulfilled for something else to be possible.

e.g. *He had been banned from drinking alcohol as a condition of bail.*

precondition prerequisite provision proviso requirement rider rule stipulation terms

conference

(noun) A conference is a meeting at which formal discussions take place.

e.g. *a conference on housing.*

congress convention forum meeting symposium

confess

(verb) If you confess to something, you admit it.

e.g. *Your son has confessed to his crimes.*

acknowledge admit come clean *informal* own up

confession

(noun) If you make a confession, you admit you have done something wrong.

e.g. *a confession of failure.*

acknowledgment admission

confidence

(noun) Someone who has confidence is sure of their own abilities, qualities, or ideas.

e.g. *I could speak with confidence.*

aplomb assurance certainty conviction self-assurance self-possession

confident

1. (adjective) If you are confident about something, you are sure it will happen the way you want it to.

e.g. *They are confident that demand will grow.*

certain convinced positive satisfied sure

2. People who are confident are sure of their own abilities, qualities, or ideas.

e.g. *John sounded powerful and confident.*

assured self-assured self-possessed

confirm

(verb) To confirm something means to say or show that it is true.

e.g. *Police later confirmed that they had received a call.*

authenticate bear out corroborate endorse ratify substantiate validate verify

confirmed

(adjective) You use confirmed to describe someone who has a habit, belief, or way of life that is unlikely to change.

e.g. *a confirmed bachelor.*

chronic habitual hardened inveterate seasoned

conflict

1. (noun) Conflict is disagreement and argument.

e.g. *conflict between workers and management.*

antagonism clash contention disagreement discord dissension fight friction hostility strife

2. When there is a conflict of ideas or interests, people have

different ideas or interests which cannot all be satisfied.
e.g. *a conflict of loyalties.*
clash difference opposition variance

3. (verb) When ideas or interests conflict, they are different and cannot all be satisfied.
e.g. *Fear and curiosity conflicted within me.*
be at variance clash collide differ disagree

conform

(verb) If something conforms to a law or to someone's wishes, it is what is required or wanted.
e.g. *His refusal to conform earned him a reputation as a troublemaker.*
comply fit in with follow go along with obey yield

confuse

(verb) To confuse someone means to make them uncertain about what is happening or what to do.
e.g. *The riddle's purpose was to confuse us.*
baffle bewilder flummox fuddle mystify perplex puzzle

congeal

(verb) When a liquid congeals, it becomes very thick and sticky.
e.g. *The blood had started to congeal.*
clot coagulate curdle

conscience

(noun) Your conscience is the part of your mind that tells you what is right and wrong.
e.g. *Some criminals have a conscience.*
principles scruples

conscientious

(adjective) Someone who is conscientious is very careful to do their work properly.
e.g. *a very conscientious student.*

careful dedicated diligent meticulous painstaking particular punctilious scrupulous thorough

consider

(verb) To consider something means to think about it carefully.

e.g. *If an offer were made, we would consider it.*

contemplate deliberate mull over muse ponder reflect ruminate think about weigh

consideration

(noun) Consideration is careful thought about something.

e.g. *a decision demanding careful consideration.*

contemplation deliberation examination perusal reflection scrutiny study thought

consist

(verb) What something consists of is its different parts or members.

e.g. *The brain consists of millions of nerve cells.*

be composed of be made up of comprise contain

constant

(adjective) If an amount or level is constant, it stays the same.

e.g. *a constant temperature.*

consistent even fixed immutable regular stable steady unchanging uniform

consult

1. (verb) If you consult someone, you ask for their opinion or advice.

e.g. *If you feel pain, consult your doctor.*

ask take counsel

2. When people consult each other, they exchange ideas and opinions.

e.g. *They consulted with fellow officers.*

ask confer debate take counsel

consume

(verb) To consume fuel or energy means to use it up.

e.g. *Running consumes a tremendous amount of energy.*

absorb eat up exhaust expend spend use up wear out

contact

(verb) If you contact someone, you telephone them or write to them.

e.g. *Where can I contact him?*

get hold of get in touch with reach

container

(noun) A container is something such as a box or a bottle that you keep things in.

e.g. *a container for water.*

holder receptacle repository vessel

contest

(noun) A contest is a competition or game.

e.g. *a boxing contest.*

championship competition game match tournament trial

contestant

(noun) The contestants in a competition are the people taking part in it.

e.g. *contestants on quiz shows.*

candidate competitor contender entrant participant player

contingent

(noun) A contingent is a group of people representing a country or organization.

e.g. *a strong British contingent.*

body delegation deputation detachment lobby

continual

1. (adjective) happening all the time without stopping.

e.g. *continual headaches.*

constant continuous endless eternal everlasting incessant interminable nonstop perpetual persistent unceasing unremitting

2. happening again and again.

e.g. *the continual snide remarks.*

constant continuous endless eternal everlasting frequent incessant interminable nonstop perpetual persistent recurrent regular repeated unceasing unremitting

continuation

1. (noun) The continuation of something is the continuing of it.

e.g. *the continuation of war.*

perpetuation prolongation

2. Something that is a continuation of an event follows it and seems like a part of it.

e.g. *a continuation of his earlier music.*

extension sequel supplement

continue

1. (verb) If you continue to do something, you keep doing it.

e.g. *Hanley continued to read his book.*

carry on go on keep on persist

2. You also say something continues when it starts again after stopping.

e.g. *She continued after a pause.*

carry on go on proceed recommence resume

contribute

(verb) If you contribute money, you give it to help to pay for something.

e.g. *He contributes generously to the Conservative Party.*

chip in *informal* donate give subscribe

control

(verb) If you control yourself, you make yourself behave calmly when you are angry or upset.

e.g. *Unable to control myself, I started shouting.*

check constrain contain curb hold back restrain

controversial

(adjective) Something that is controversial causes a lot of discussion and argument, because many people disapprove of it.

e.g. *controversial ideas.*

contentious outrageous provocative

convenient

(adjective) If something is convenient, it is easy to use or it makes something easy to do.

e.g. *a convenient meeting place.*

handy helpful labour-saving opportune seasonable suitable timely useful well-timed

convince

(verb) To convince someone of something means to persuade them that it is true.

e.g. *I convinced him you could be trusted.*

assure persuade prove to satisfy sway win over

convincing

(adjective) Convincing is used to describe things or people that can make you believe something is true.

e.g. *a convincing argument.*

believable cogent credible persuasive plausible powerful telling

copy

1. (noun) A copy is something made to look like something else.

e.g. *a good copy of her signature.*

counterfeit duplicate facsimile forgery image imitation

likeness replica reproduction

2. (verb) If you copy what someone does, you do the same thing.
e.g. *Children learn from copying their parents.*
ape follow imitate mimic

3. If you copy something, you make a copy of it.
e.g. *He copied the chart from a book.*
counterfeit duplicate photocopy replicate reproduce

corny

(adjective) very obvious or sentimental and not at all original.
e.g. *corny old love songs.*
banal hackneyed old-fashioned sentimental stale trite

correct

1. (adjective) If something is correct, there are no mistakes in it.
e.g. *The first correct answer we receive will win the prize.*
accurate exact faultless flawless precise right true

2. (verb) If you correct something which is wrong, you make it right.
e.g. *She corrected my grammar.*
adjust amend cure emend improve rectify redress reform remedy right

corrupt

1. (adjective) Corrupt people act dishonestly or illegally in return for money or power.
e.g. *corrupt ministers.*
bent *slang* crooked *informal* dishonest fraudulent rotten shady unethical unprincipled unscrupulous

2. (verb) To corrupt someone means to make them dishonest or immoral.
e.g. *Power has totally corrupted him.*
bribe debauch deprave pervert

corruption

(noun; a formal use) Corruption is immoral sexual behaviour.

e.g. *a war against corruption and other vices.*

debauchery decadence degeneration depravity immorality impurity perversion vice viciousness wickedness

count

1. (verb) If you count all the things in a group, you add them up to see how many there are.

e.g. *He counted the number of steps.*

calculate compute enumerate number reckon tally tot up

2. (noun) A count is a number reached by counting.

e.g. *The final count is going to be high.*

calculation computation enumeration reckoning score tally

countless

(adjective) too many to count.

e.g. *There had been countless demonstrations.*

endless incalculable infinite innumerable legion myriad *literary* untold

country

(noun) A country is one of the political areas the world is divided into.

e.g. *the country of New Zealand.*

kingdom land nation realm state

county

(noun) A county is a region with its own local government.

e.g. *the remote county of Devon.*

province shire

coup

(noun) When there is a coup, a group of people seize power in a country.

e.g. *A coup almost overthrew the government.*

coup d'état overthrow takeover

course

(noun) A course is a piece of land where a sport such as golf is played.

e.g. *a motor racing course.*

circuit racecourse track

cower

(verb) When someone cowers, they crouch or move backwards because they are afraid.

e.g. *Men were cowering behind vehicles.*

cringe crouch quail shrink

crack

(noun) A crack is a narrow gap.

e.g. *a deep crack in the ceiling.*

breach break chink cleft cranny crevice fissure fracture gap rift split

cram

(verb) If you cram people or things into a place, you put more in than there is room for.

e.g. *People were crammed into the flats.*

compress crowd force jam overcrowd pack pack in press shove squeeze stuff

craze

(noun) A craze is something that is very popular for a short time.

e.g. *a new fashion craze.*

cult fad fashion mania trend vogue

credible

(adjective) If someone or something is credible, you can believe or trust them.

e.g. *a credible alternative leader.*

believable conceivable imaginable likely plausible possible

creep

(verb) To creep means to move quietly and slowly.

e.g. *I crept back into the kitchen.*

skulk slink sneak steal tiptoe

creepy

(adjective; an informal word) strange and frightening.

e.g. *He could not get rid of that creepy feeling.*

eerie frightening scary *informal* sinister spooky

crime

(noun) A crime is an action for which you can be punished by law.

e.g. *a serious crime.*

felony misdeed misdemeanour offence transgression violation wrong wrongdoing

criminal

(noun) A criminal is someone who has committed a crime.

e.g. *a very dangerous criminal.*

crook culprit felon offender transgressor wrongdoer villain

cripple

(verb) To cripple someone means to injure them severely so that they can never move properly again.

e.g. *The blast crippled her.*

disable lame maim paralyse

critical

1. (adjective) A critical time is one which is very important in determining what happens in the future.

e.g. *a critical point in his career.*

crucial decisive momentous pivotal vital

2. A critical situation is a very serious one.

e.g. *The economy is in a critical state.*

dangerous grave perilous precarious serious

3. If you are critical of something or someone, you criticize them.

e.g. *His critical attitude puts a lot of people off.*

carping cavilling censorious derogatory disparaging scathing

criticize

(verb) If you criticize someone or something, you say what you think is wrong with them.

e.g. *My parents criticized me endlessly.*

censure condemn disparage find fault with
knock *informal* put down slag *informal* slate *informal*

cross

1. (verb) If you cross something such as a room or a road, you go to the other side of it.

e.g. *He crossed over to the phone.*

bridge ford go across span traverse

2. Lines or roads that cross meet and go across each other.

e.g. *The pipe crossed under the road.*

crisscross intersect meet

3. (noun) Something that is a cross between two things is neither one thing nor the other, but a mixture of both.

e.g. *a cross between a donkey and a horse.*

blend combination crossbreed hybrid mixture mongrel

crouch

(verb) If you are crouching, you are leaning forward with your legs bent under you.

e.g. *I crouched down behind the chair.*

bend down huddle hunch squat

crowd

(noun) A crowd is a large group of people gathered together.

e.g. *A crowd gathered outside.*

bevy flock horde host mob multitude swarm throng

crucial

(adjective) If something is crucial, it is very important in determining how something else will be in the future.

e.g. *a crucial role to play.*

central critical decisive pivotal vital

crude

1. (adjective) rough and simple.

e.g. *a crude weapon.*

clumsy makeshift primitive rough rudimentary simple unrefined

2. A crude person speaks or behaves in a rude and offensive way.

e.g. *You can be quite crude at times.*

boorish coarse crass dirty gross indecent indelicate lewd obscene ribald rough rude smutty tasteless uncouth vulgar

cruel

(adjective) Cruel people deliberately cause pain or distress to other people or to animals.

e.g. *a cruel husband.*

brutal callous cold-blooded hard heartless inhuman inhumane merciless pitiless remorseless sadistic unkind vicious

crumple

(verb) To crumple paper or cloth means to squash it so that it is full of creases and folds.

e.g. *He crumpled up the paper and tossed it away.*

crease crush rumple screw up

cry

(verb) When you cry, tears appear in your eyes.

e.g. *She was crying so much she could hardly speak.*

bawl blubber snivel sob wail weep

cunning

1. (adjective) Someone who is cunning uses clever and deceitful methods to get what they want.

e.g. *a cunning lawyer.*

artful canny crafty devious foxy sharp shifty sly tricky wily

2. (noun) Cunning is the ability to get what you want using clever and deceitful methods.

e.g. *She's got the cunning of a weasel.*

craftiness deviousness guile slyness wiliness

cure

1. (verb) To cure an illness means to end it.

e.g. *a means of curing the common cold.*

heal remedy

2. To cure a sick or injured person means to make them well.

e.g. *He cured me of hepatitis.*

heal mend restore

curiosity

(noun) A curiosity is something unusual and interesting.

e.g. *This stuffed turtle is a curiosity.*

curio novelty oddity rarity

curious

(adjective) Someone who is curious wants to know more about something.

e.g. *He is terribly curious about people.*

inquiring inquisitive interested nosey prying

custom

1. (noun) A custom is a traditional activity.

e.g. *an ancient Chinese custom.*

convention practice ritual tradition way

2. A custom is also something usually done at a particular time or in particular circumstances by a person or by the people in a society.

e.g. *It was also my custom to do Christmas shows.*

habit manner practice procedure routine way wont

customer

(noun) A shop's or firm's customers are the people who buy its goods.

e.g. *the customer of a bank.*

buyer client consumer patron purchaser shopper

cut

1. (verb) If you cut something, you use a knife, scissors, or some other sharp tool to mark it, damage it, or remove parts of it.

e.g. *Cut the butter into small pieces.*

clip lacerate nick score sever slash slice slit

2. If you cut yourself, you injure yourself on a sharp object.

e.g. *I cut my hand.*

gash lacerate nick slash slit wound

3. (noun) A cut is an injury caused by a sharp object.

e.g. *The cut was so deep it needed stitches.*

gash incision laceration nick slash slit wound

D d

danger

(noun) Danger is the possibility that someone may be harmed or killed.

e.g. *There was widespread danger of disease.*

hazard jeopardy menace peril risk threat

dangerous

(adjective) able to or likely to cause hurt or harm.

e.g. *a very dangerous situation.*

hazardous menacing perilous risky threatening treacherous unsafe

dapper

(adjective) neat and smart in appearance.

e.g. *a dapper fellow in a black velvet jacket.*

natty neat smart spruce spry stylish trim well-groomed

dark

(adjective) If it is dark, there is not enough light to see properly.

e.g. *It was very dark in the tunnel.*

cloudy dim dusky gloomy murky overcast shadowy sombre unlit

dazed

(adjective) If you are dazed, you are stunned and unable to think clearly.

e.g. *I was too dazed to say or do anything.*

bemused bewildered confused dizzy dopey *informal* fuddled light-headed muddled stunned stupefied

deadlock

(noun) A deadlock is a situation in which neither side in a dispute is willing to give in.

e.g. *The talks ended in deadlock.*

impasse stalemate

dear

1. (adjective) much loved.

e.g. *a very dear friend.*

beloved cherished close esteemed intimate precious

2. Something that is dear is very expensive.

e.g. *I can't afford it, it's too dear.*

costly expensive pricey *informal*

debatable

(adjective) not absolutely certain.

e.g. *The justness of these wars is debatable.*

arguable borderline controversial disputable doubtful dubious questionable uncertain

decent

(adjective) Decent people are honest and respectable.

e.g. *He seemed to be a decent man.*

decorous nice polite presentable proper respectable seemly

deceptive

(adjective) likely to make people believe something that is not true.

e.g. *Appearances can be deceptive.*

ambiguous deceitful false illusory misleading mock

decide

1. (verb) If you decide to do something, you choose to do it.

e.g. *I decided to stay on and fight.*

choose determine elect resolve

2. If an event or fact decides a situation, it makes a particular result or choice absolutely certain.
e.g. *The cup final was decided on penalties.*
adjudicate conclude end settle

decision

(noun) A decision is a choice or judgment that is made about something.
e.g. *The editor's decision is final.*
conclusion judgment resolution ruling settlement verdict

declaration

(noun) A declaration is a firm, forceful statement, often an official announcement.
e.g. *a declaration of war.*
affirmation announcement assertion promulgation pronouncement statement

declare

(verb) If you declare something, you say it firmly and forcefully.
e.g *He declared he was going to be famous.*
affirm announce assert aver avow claim maintain proclaim pronounce state

decorate

(verb) If you decorate something, you make it more attractive by adding some ornament or colour to it.
e.g. *Antonia decorated the cake with cream.*
adorn beautify deck embellish festoon garnish ornament trim

dedicate

(verb) If you dedicate yourself to something, you devote your time and energy to it.
e.g. *He dedicates himself to golf.*
commit devote pledge surrender

deduce

(verb) If you deduce something, you work it out from other facts that you know are true.

e.g. *He deduced that there had been an argument.*

conclude gather infer reason surmise understand

defile

(verb) To defile something precious or holy means to spoil or damage it.

e.g. *The graves were defiled by vandals.*

desecrate profane

deform

(verb) To deform something means to put it out of shape or spoil its appearance.

e.g. *Badly fitting shoes can deform the feet.*

cripple disfigure distort maim twist warp

defy

(verb) If you defy a person or a law, you openly resist and refuse to obey.

e.g. *He defied doctor's orders.*

challenge confront dare flout scorn slight

degrade

(verb) If something degrades people, it humiliates or corrupts them.

e.g. *My grandfather always said that work degraded men.*

corrupt debase demean discredit disgrace pervert shame

dejected

(adjective) miserable and unhappy.

e.g. *Dejected prisoners sat in rows.*

crestfallen depressed despondent disconsolate disheartened downcast gloomy morose sad wretched

delay

(verb) If you delay doing something, you put it off until a later time.

e.g. *I delayed my decision.*

defer postpone procrastinate put off suspend temporize

delete

(verb) To delete something written means to rub it out or remove it.

e.g. *I got permission to delete the whole entry.*

cancel cross out erase expunge obliterate remove rub out

deliberate

(adjective) intentional or planned in advance.

e.g. *It was a deliberate insult.*

calculated conscious considered intentional knowing planned premeditated studied wilful

delicious

(adjective) very pleasing, especially to taste.

e.g. *delicious fruit.*

appetizing choice delectable luscious mouthwatering savoury scrumptious tasty

demanding

(adjective) requiring a lot of time, energy, or attention.

e.g. *He has a demanding job.*

challenging difficult exacting taxing tough

demonstrative

(adjective) People who are demonstrative openly show or express their feelings.

e.g. *They are unusually demonstrative and affectionate with their friends.*

effusive gushing unreserved

deny

(verb) If you deny something that has been said, you state that it is untrue.

e.g. *Powell denied reports that he had threatened to resign.*

contradict gainsay repudiate

depend

(verb) If you depend on someone or something, you trust them and rely on them.

e.g. *You can depend on me.*

bank on count on rely on trust

dependable

(adjective) reliable and trustworthy.

e.g. *He was dependable and loyal.*

faithful reliable staunch steady sure trustworthy trusty unfailing

dependent

(adjective) reliant on someone or something.

e.g. *Many countries are almost entirely dependent on tourism.*

conditional contingent on helpless provisional reliant subject to vulnerable

depressed

(adjective) unhappy and gloomy.

e.g. *I have been feeling depressed about work.*

despondent dispirited doleful down downcast fed up *informal* glum low melancholy sad unhappy

deserve

(verb) If you deserve something, you are entitled to it or earn it because of your qualities, achievements, or actions.

e.g. *He deserved a rest.*

earn justify merit rate warrant

deserving

(adjective) worthy of being helped, rewarded, or praised.
e.g. *a deserving charity.*
commendable meritorious praiseworthy worthy

desire

1. (verb) If you desire something, you want it very much.
e.g. *I desired to expand the business.*
covet crave fancy hanker after want wish

2. (noun) A desire is a strong feeling of wanting something.
e.g. *a desire to be rich.*
appetite craving hankering longing lust need thirst want

despair

(noun) Despair is a total loss of hope.
e.g. *He felt a sense of despair at his own stupidity.*
anguish desperation hopelessness

despite

(preposition) in spite of.
e.g. *He fell asleep despite all the coffee he'd drunk.*
in spite of irrespective of notwithstanding regardless of

destitute

(adjective) without money or possessions, and therefore in great need.
e.g. *St Anne's was established to house destitute children.*
down-and-out impecunious impoverished insolvent needy penniless penurious poor

destroy

(verb) To destroy something means to damage it so much that it is completely ruined.
e.g. *A fire destroyed most of the house.*
annihilate demolish devastate exterminate obliterate

raze ruin shatter wipe out wreck

destruction

(noun) Destruction is the act of destroying something or the state of being destroyed.

e.g. *the destruction of the rainforest.*

annihilation demolition devastation downfall end extermination extinction obliteration overthrow ruin wrecking

determine

1. (verb) To determine something means to decide or settle it firmly.

e.g. *The date has still to be determined.*

decide establish settle

2. To determine something means to find out or calculate the facts about it.

e.g. *He bit the coin to determine whether it was genuine.*

ascertain check detect discover find out learn verify work out

determined

(adjective) firmly decided.

e.g. *She was determined not to repeat her error.*

adamant dogged firm intent on resolute single-minded steadfast tenacious

dictator

(noun) A dictator is a ruler who has complete power in a country, especially one who has taken power by force.

e.g. *the grim rule of the ruthless dictator.*

autocrat despot oppressor tyrant

diction

(noun) Someone's diction is the clarity with which they speak or sing.

e.g. *a quiet, even-toned voice with perfect diction.*
articulation delivery enunciation intonation pronunciation speech

die

(verb) When people, animals, or plants die, they stop living.
e.g. *Sir Malcolm died in 1948.*
disappear expire pass away perish vanish

difference

(noun) The difference between things is the way in which they are unlike each other.
e.g. *the difference between butter and margarine.*
contrast discrepancy disparity dissimilarity distinction divergence variation

different

1. (adjective) unlike something else.
e.g. *France is very different from England.*
contrasting disparate dissimilar divergent unlike

2. distinct and separate, although of the same kind.
e.g. *The lunch supports different charities each year.*
alternative assorted diverse sundry variant varied various

difficult

1. (adjective) not easy to do, understand, or solve.
e.g. *He was doing a difficult job.*
demanding formidable hard knotty laborious onerous thorny tricky uphill

2. hard to deal with or troublesome, especially because of being unreasonable or unpredictable.
e.g. *a difficult child.*
awkward fractious perverse tiresome troublesome trying unmanageable

difficulty

(noun) A difficulty is a problem.

e.g. *If Mr. Dayton were in some kind of difficulty, who else might he phone?*

fix *informal* jam *informal* mess pickle *informal* plight predicament spot *informal* trouble

dilapidated

(adjective) falling to pieces and generally in a bad condition.

e.g. *They had renovated the house from a very dilapidated condition.*

broken down decayed decaying decrepit neglected ramshackle rickety run down

diligent

(adjective) hard-working, and showing care and perseverance.

e.g. *a diligent student.*

assiduous conscientious indefatigable industrious studious tireless

direct

(adjective) straightforward, and without delay or evasion.

e.g. *his direct and abrupt manner.*

candid forthright frank matter-of-fact outspoken straight straightforward

dirt

(noun) Dirt is any unclean substance, such as dust, mud, or stains.

e.g. *His face was streaked with dirt.*

filth grime impurity muck squalor

dirty

(adjective) marked or covered with dirt.

e.g. *dirty clothes.*

filthy foul grimy grotty *slang* grubby messy mucky polluted soiled

disadvantage

(noun) A disadvantage is an unfavourable or harmful circumstance.

e.g. *the double disadvantage of being deaf and dumb.*

detriment drawback handicap hindrance liability minus

disagree

(verb) If you disagree with someone, you have a different view or opinion from theirs.

e.g. *Lord Morton disagreed with Lord Prosser.*

argue bicker clash differ dissent diverge quarrel wrangle

disappear

(verb) To disappear means to stop existing or happening.

e.g. *The pain has disappeared.*

cease dissolve end evaporate fade melt away pass away vanish wane

disaster

1. (noun) A disaster is an event or accident that causes great distress or destruction.

e.g. *a major rail disaster.*

accident blow calamity cataclysm catastrophe misfortune tragedy

2. A disaster is also a complete failure.

e.g. *The family holiday in Majorca was a disaster.*

catastrophe debacle fiasco

discard

(verb) To discard something means to get rid of it, because you no longer want it or find it useful.

e.g. *Scoop out the seeds and discard them.*

abandon dispose of ditch *slang* drop dump *informal* jettison scrap shed

discerning

(adjective) having good taste and judgment.

e.g. *a discerning collector.*

discriminating judicious perceptive perspicacious selective shrewd

discourage

(verb) To discourage someone means to take away their enthusiasm or confidence to do something.

e.g. *Uncle Alfred discouraged me from writing poetry.*

dampen dash daunt demoralize deter dishearten dismay intimidate

discussion

(noun) A discussion is a conversation or piece of writing in which a subject is considered in detail, from several points of view.

e.g. *a discussion about football.*

consultation debate dialogue discourse exchange

disgrace

1. (noun) Disgrace is loss of approval and respect by people towards another person.

e.g. *She had brought disgrace to her family.*

discredit disfavour dishonour disrepute humiliation ignominy infamy opprobrium shame stigma

2. (verb) If you disgrace yourself or disgrace someone else, you cause yourself or them to be strongly disapproved of by other people.

e.g. *scenes that have disgraced the game of cricket.*

discredit dishonour humiliate shame

disgraceful

(adjective) If something is disgraceful, people disapprove of it strongly and think that those who are responsible for it should be ashamed.

e.g. *I complained about his disgraceful behaviour.*

contemptible discreditable dishonourable disreputable infamous outrageous reprehensible scandalous shameful shocking

disgust

1. (noun) Disgust is the feeling aroused in you by something that is morally wrong, shameful, or very unpleasant.

e.g. *The book left her with a strong feeling of disgust.*

abhorrence antipathy detestation distaste loathing repugnance repulsion revulsion

2. (verb) To disgust someone means to make them feel sickened and disapproving.

e.g. *The idea disgusted me.*

displease nauseate offend outrage put off repel revolt sicken

disgusting

(adjective) very unpleasant and offensive.

e.g. *The food was disgusting.*

abominable foul gross hateful loathsome nasty nauseating odious offensive repellent repugnant repulsive revolting sickening vile

dislike

(noun) Dislike is a feeling that you have when you do not like someone or something.

e.g. *his dislike of men with beards.*

animosity antagonism antipathy aversion detestation disapproval disgust distaste enmity hatred hostility loathing repugnance

disorder

(noun) Disorder is a lack of organization.

e.g. *The men fled in disorder.*

bedlam chaos confusion disorganization mayhem shambles turmoil

distant

(adjective) Someone who is distant is cold and unfriendly.

e.g. *He adopted a very distant attitude.*

aloof cold cool formal haughty reserved standoffish stiff unapproachable withdrawn

distasteful

(adjective) If you find something distasteful, you think it is unpleasant or offensive.

e.g. *I find her gossip distasteful.*

abhorrent disagreeable displeasing obnoxious offensive repugnant repulsive unpalatable unpleasant unsavoury

distract

(verb) If something distracts you, your attention is taken away from what you are doing.

e.g. *A disturbance in the street distracted my attention.*

divert sidetrack

distress

1. (noun) Distress is great suffering.

e.g. *He was in a state of extreme distress when she left him.*

affliction agony anguish anxiety desolation discomfort grief heartache misery pain sadness sorrow torment

2. (verb) To distress someone means to make them feel alarmed or unhappy.

e.g. *Her death had profoundly distressed me.*

afflict disturb grieve harrow pain sadden upset worry wound

distressing

(adjective) very worrying or upsetting.

e.g. *a distressing new report.*

affecting disturbing harrowing heart-rending painful sad upsetting

distribute

(verb) To distribute something means to divide it and share it out among a number of people.

e.g. *Organisers plan to distribute posters and leaflets.*

assign dispense divide dole out give out share out

disturb

(verb) If something disturbs you, it makes you feel upset or worried.

e.g. *The atmosphere disturbed her.*

agitate alarm disconcert distress fluster perturb ruffle shake trouble unnerve unsettle upset worry

dive

(verb) If an aircraft or bird dives, it flies in a steep downward path, or drops sharply.

e.g. *His plane stalled and dived into the ground.*

dip plummet plunge swoop

dizzy

(adjective) having or causing a whirling sensation.

e.g. *He felt sick and dizzy and then passed out.*

dazed faint giddy light-headed reeling shaky staggering swimming wobbly

do

(verb) If someone does a task, chore, or activity, they perform it and finish it.

e.g. *He just didn't want to do any work.*

accomplish achieve carry out complete conclude discharge effect execute perform

doubt

(noun) Doubt is a feeling of uncertainty about whether something is true or possible.

e.g. *There was some doubt about whether the pistol was loaded.*

disquiet distrust dubiety fear misgiving mistrust qualm reservation scepticism suspicion uncertainty

downpour

(noun) A downpour is a heavy fall of rain.

e.g. *Banana plantations were drenched by the downpour.*

cloudburst deluge flood inundation

drab

(adjective) dull and unattractive.

e.g. *a drab grey suit.*

colourless dingy dismal dreary dull flat lacklustre sombre

drag

(verb) If you drag a heavy object somewhere, you pull it slowly and with difficulty.

e.g. *Four men dragged the driver from his cab.*

draw haul lug pull tow trail tug yank

drastic

(adjective) A drastic course of action is very strong and severe and is usually taken urgently.

e.g. *drastic measures to cut unemployment.*

desperate dramatic extreme harsh radical severe strong

dreadful

(adjective) very bad or unpleasant.

e.g. *She had dreadful nightmares.*

abominable abysmal appalling atrocious deplorable frightful ghastly hideous horrible monstrous shocking terrible

drink

1. (verb) When you drink, you take liquid into your mouth and swallow it.

e.g. *You should drink plenty of water.*
drain gulp imbibe sip swallow swig *informal*

2. To drink also means to drink alcohol.
e.g. *He drinks little and eats carefully.*
booze *informal* imbibe tipple

drudgery

(noun) Drudgery is hard uninteresting work.
e.g. *I hate the drudgery of paperwork.*
chore donkey-work grind labour slavery slog *informal* toil

drunk

(adjective) If someone is drunk, they have drunk so much alcohol that they cannot speak clearly or behave sensibly.
e.g. *His son was killed by a drunk driver.*
drunken fuddled inebriated intoxicated merry *informal* sloshed *slang* tight *informal* tipsy

dry

(adjective) Something that is dry contains or uses no water or liquid.
e.g. *a dry cloth.*
arid barren dehydrated parched thirsty

dubious

(adjective) not entirely honest, safe, or reliable.
e.g. *dubious sales techniques.*
dodgy *informal* doubtful questionable suspect suspicious

dull

1. (adjective) not at all interesting.
e.g. *She thought the book dull and unoriginal.*
boring commonplace dreary dry flat plain prosaic tedious

2. A dull day or a dull sky is very cloudy.

e.g. *The weather was generally dull and rainy.*
cloudy gloomy heavy leaden overcast

dumb

(adjective) unable to speak.
e.g. *I was dumb with shyness and awe.*
mute silent soundless speechless

duty

(noun) Duties are things you ought to do or feel you should do, because it is your responsibility to do them.
e.g. *We have a duty as adults to listen to children.*
function obligation responsibility role task

E e

early

1. (adverb) before the arranged or expected time.

e.g. *They arrived early.*

ahead of time   prematurely   too soon

2. (adjective) happening before the arranged or expected time.

e.g. *We had an early dinner.*

premature   untimely

earn

(verb) If you earn money, you get it in return for work that you do.

e.g. *As a top model Clare earned a fortune.*

bring in   gain   get   gross   make   obtain   receive

ease

1. (noun) Ease is lack of difficulty, worry, or hardship.

e.g. *He had sailed through life with relative ease.*

comfort   contentment   easiness   enjoyment   facility   leisure

2. (verb) When something eases, or when you ease it, it becomes less.

e.g. *She took an aspirin to ease her headache.*

abate   alleviate   assuage   lessen   lighten   moderate   relieve

easy

(adjective) able to be done without difficulty.

e.g. *This book is short and easy to read.*

effortless   light   simple   straightforward   undemanding

easy-going

(adjective) not easily annoyed or worried.

e.g. *He had a reputation as an easy-going boss.*

calm laid-back *informal* placid relaxed tolerant

eccentric

1. (adjective) having habits or opinions which other people think are odd or peculiar.

e.g. *an eccentric professor.*

bizarre cranky odd outlandish peculiar queer quirky strange unconventional weird

2. (noun) An eccentric is someone who is eccentric.

e.g. *Artists are notorious eccentrics.*

crank oddball *informal* weirdo *informal*

economy

(noun) Economy is the careful use of things to save money, time, or energy.

e.g. *For economy, steel tables are used on cheaper models.*

frugality husbandry saving thrift

ecstasy

(noun) Ecstasy is a feeling of extreme happiness.

e.g. *He jumped up and down in ecstasy.*

bliss delight elation euphoria exaltation joy rapture

edge

(noun) The edge of something is a border or line where it ends or meets something else.

e.g. *a motel on the edge of a lake.*

border boundary brink fringe limit margin perimeter rim side

efficient

(adjective) capable of doing something well without wasting time or energy.

e.g. *an efficient secretary.*

able adept businesslike capable competent proficient skilful well-organized workmanlike

effort

(noun) Effort is the physical or mental energy needed to do something.

e.g. *Her face screwed up with effort.*

energy exertion labour pains striving toil trouble work

eject

(verb) If you eject something or someone, you forcefully push or send them out.

e.g. *The pod was ejected from the spacecraft.*

discharge emit expel throw out

elaborate

1. (adjective) highly decorated and complicated.

e.g. *elaborate designs.*

complex complicated decorated detailed fussy intricate ornamented ornate

2. (verb) If you elaborate on something, you add more information or detail about it.

e.g. *Dr Bing would not elaborate on the events.*

add detail amplify embellish expand

embarrass

(verb) If you embarrass someone, you make them feel shy, ashamed, or uncomfortable.

e.g. *He had never sought to embarrass her by referring to the incident.*

discomfit disconcert humiliate mortify shame show up *informal*

emergency

(noun) An emergency is an unexpected and serious event which needs immediate action to deal with it.

e.g. *I had a friend nearby who could help out in an emergency.*

crisis difficulty exigency extremity necessity plight predicament

emit

(verb) To emit something means to give it out or release it.

e.g. *The food emitted a strong smell.*

discharge emanate exude give off give out issue

employ

(verb) If you employ someone, you pay them to work for you.

e.g. *The company employs eighteen staff.*

engage enlist hire take on

empty

1. (adjective) having nothing or nobody inside.

e.g. *an empty house.*

bare blank hollow unfurnished uninhabited unoccupied vacant void

2. without purpose, value, or meaning.

e.g. *empty gestures.*

aimless hollow meaningless worthless

3. (verb) If you empty something, or empty its contents, you remove the contents.

e.g. *I emptied my kitchen cupboards.*

clear vacate void

encourage

(verb) If you encourage someone, you give them courage and confidence to do something.

e.g. *Naomi encouraged her to train as a nurse.*

buoy up egg on embolden incite inspire urge

end

(noun) The end of something is the farthest point of it.

e.g. *the room at the end of the passage.*

boundary edge extremity limit tip

endanger

(verb) To endanger something means to cause it to be in a dangerous and harmful situation.

e.g. *Insecticides can endanger wildlife.*

imperil jeopardize put at risk threaten

enemy

(noun) An enemy is a person or group that is hostile or opposed to another person or group.

e.g. *He had many enemies in London.*

adversary antagonist foe opponent

energetic

(adjective) having or showing energy or enthusiasm.

e.g. *thousands of energetic volunteers.*

active alive brisk dynamic lively spirited tireless vigorous

energy

(noun) Energy is the physical strength to do active things.

e.g. *Bill is a man with boundless energy and enthusiasm.*

drive force go *informal* power stamina strength verve vigour

engross

(verb) If something or someone engrosses you, they hold all your attention.

e.g. *She was engrossed in her book.*

absorb immerse involve

entertain

(verb) If you entertain people, you keep them amused, interested, or attentive.

e.g. *He entertained us with wonderful stories.*

amuse divert occupy

enthusiasm

(noun) Enthusiasm is interest, eagerness, or delight in something that you enjoy.

e.g. *a passionate enthusiasm for sport.*

ardour eagerness fervour gusto interest keenness passion relish zeal zest

entrance

(verb) If something entrances you, it gives you a feeling of wonder and delight.

e.g. *He was immediately entranced by her voice.*

captivate charm enchant enthral fascinate

entry

1. (noun) Entry is the act of entering a place.

e.g. *The thieves gained entry by smashing the window.*

access admission admittance entrance

2. An entry is also any place through which you enter somewhere.

e.g. *the entry to the main room.*

door doorway entrance gate way in

equal

(verb) If one thing equals another, it is as good or remarkable as the other.

e.g. *Nobody can equal her skill at the piano.*

match parallel rival

equality

(noun) Equality is the same status, rights, and responsibilities for all members of a society.

e.g. *There should be equality of opportunity for all.*

equivalence fairness parity

equip

(verb) If a person or thing is equipped with something, they have it or are provided with it.

e.g. *We were well equipped for the journey.*

fit out furnish kit out provide stock supply

equipment

(noun) Equipment is all the things that are needed or used for a particular job or activity.

e.g. *photographic equipment.*

accoutrements apparatus gear kit paraphernalia stuff tackle

equivalent

(noun) An equivalent is something that has the same use, size, value, or effect as something else.

e.g. *Lieutenant Commander is the Navy equivalent to an Army Major.*

counterpart equal match parallel

era

(noun) An era is a period of time distinguished by a particular feature.

e.g. *the jazz era of the '20s.*

age epoch period time

erect

(adjective) in a straight and upright position.

e.g. *The hairs stand erect to retain more body heat.*

standing straight upright vertical

err

(verb) If you err, you make a mistake.
e.g. *To err is human.*
blunder miscalculate slip up

essence

(noun) The essence of something is the perfect form of it.
e.g. *the essence of a British summer.*
quintessence soul spirit

establish

(verb) To establish something means to create it or set it up in a permanent way.
e.g. *He has established a successful business.*
create found institute set up start

eternal

(adjective) lasting forever, or seeming to last forever.
e.g. *his eternal complaints.*
abiding constant endless everlasting perpetual unending

etiquette

(noun) Etiquette is a set of rules for behaviour in a particular social situation.
e.g. *a strict observance of army etiquette.*
code customs decorum formalities manners propriety protocol

even

1. (adjective) flat and level.
e.g. *an even layer of chocolate.*
flat horizontal level smooth straight

2. Scores that are even are exactly the same.
e.g. *Honours were even.*
equal fifty-fifty *informal* level

event

(noun) An event is something that happens, especially when it is unusual or important.

e.g. *The last great social event of the season.*

affair business episode happening incident occasion occurrence

everywhere

(adverb) in all places or to all places.

e.g. *Insects were everywhere.*

all around all over omnipresent ubiquitous

evict

(verb) To evict someone means to officially force them to leave a place they are occupying.

e.g. *She was to be evicted from her own home.*

eject expel kick out oust put out remove throw out turf out *informal*

exaggerate

(verb) To exaggerate something means to make it more noticeable than usual.

e.g. *His Irish brogue was exaggerated for the benefit of the joke he was telling.*

emphasize inflate magnify overdo overemphasize

examine

(verb) If you examine something, you inspect it very carefully.

e.g. *Police examined hospital records.*

analyse inspect investigate look over peruse scan scrutinize study survey

example

(noun) An example is something which represents or is typical of a group or set.

e.g. *some examples of early Spanish music.*

illustration instance sample specimen

excellent

(adjective) very good indeed.

e.g. *We enjoyed an excellent meal.*

admirable choice fine first-rate great masterly outstanding prime splendid superb superior superlative

excessive

(adjective) too great in amount or degree.

e.g. *using excessive force.*

extreme immoderate inordinate overdone overmuch undue

excite

(verb) If somebody or something excites you, they make you feel very happy and nervous or very interested and enthusiastic.

e.g. *I only take on work that excites me.*

electrify exhilarate inspire move rouse stimulate thrill

exclusive

(adjective) available to or for the use of a small group of rich or privileged people.

e.g. *an exclusive club.*

confined limited private restricted select

exempt

(verb) To exempt someone from a rule, duty, or obligation means to excuse them from it.

e.g. *Because of his wounded hand he was exempted from hard labour.*

absolve except excuse free let off release relieve

exercise

(verb) If you exercise your authority, rights, or responsibilities, you use them.

e.g. *I would like to exercise my right to reply.*
apply employ exert practise use utilize wield

exhaust

(verb) To exhaust someone means to make them so tired that they have no energy left.
e.g. *He was visibly exhausted by the extreme heat.*
debilitate drain enervate fatigue sap tire tire out weaken wear out weary

expand

(verb) If you expand on or expand upon something, you give more details about it.
e.g. *Claire is keen to expand on the subject.*
amplify elaborate embellish enlarge on expatiate

expanse

(noun) An expanse is a very large or widespread area.
e.g. *an expanse of sand and desert.*
area space stretch sweep tract

expect

(verb) If you expect something, you believe that it is going to happen or arrive.
e.g. *Shareholders can expect a small profit.*
anticipate assume await bargain for foresee hope for look forward to

expense

(noun) Expense is the money that something costs.
e.g. *the expense of buying electronic instruments.*
charge cost expenditure outgoings outlay

experience

(verb) If you experience a situation or feeling, it happens to you or you are affected by it.

e.g. *She experienced a growing sense of excitement.*
encounter feel go through have know meet undergo

experienced

(adjective) skilled or knowledgeable through doing something for a long time.

e.g. *an experienced sailor.*
accomplished knowledgeable practised seasoned

expert

(noun) An expert is someone who is very skilled at doing something or very knowledgeable about a particular subject.

e.g. *an expert on astrology.*
authority buff *informal* connoisseur master specialist virtuoso whiz *informal* wizard

expire

(verb) When something expires, it reaches the end of the period of time for which it is valid.

e.g. *My bus pass expires next week.*
end finish lapse run out stop terminate

explain

(verb) If you explain something, you give details about it or reasons for it so that it can be understood.

e.g. *He took them into a restaurant and explained the situation.*
clarify demonstrate elucidate expound illuminate interpret spell out

expose

(verb) To expose a person or situation means to reveal the truth about them, especially when it involves dishonest or shocking behaviour.

e.g. *Johnson was exposed as a cheat.*
bring to light debunk denounce disclose divulge reveal show up uncover unmask

extra

(adjective) more than is usual, necessary, or expected.
e.g. *an extra portion of salad.*
added additional further more supplementary

extraordinary

(adjective) unusual or surprising.
e.g. *an extraordinary feat of courage.*
exceptional phenomenal rare remarkable singular surprising uncommon unusual

F f

fabric

1. (noun) Fabric is cloth.

e.g. *a crisp cotton fabric.*

cloth   material

2. The fabric of a society or system is its structure, laws, and customs.

e.g. *The priests upheld the fabric of Roman society.*

constitution   foundations   framework   organization   structure

fabulous

1. (adjective) wonderful or very impressive.

e.g. *They missed a fabulous opportunity.*

amazing   astounding   breathtaking   immense   incredible   phenomenal

2. not real, but happening or mentioned in stories or legends.

e.g. *fabulous animals and birds.*

apocryphal   imaginary   legendary   mythical

face

(noun) Your face is the front part of your head from your chin to your forehead.

e.g. *masks which protect the face.*

countenance   features   physiognomy   visage

facility

(noun) A facility is a service, opportunity, or piece of equipment which makes it possible to do something.

e.g. *excellent shopping facilities.*

amenity   service

fact

(noun) A fact is something that is true or has actually happened.
e.g. *I don't know if the rumour is based on facts or not.*
act deed fait accompli *French* happening incident occurrence

factor

(noun) A factor is something that helps to cause a result.
e.g. *House dust mites are a major factor in asthma.*
cause component consideration element influence point

fade

(verb) If something fades, the intensity of its colour, brightness, or sound is gradually reduced.
e.g *faded photographs.*
bleach decline die out dim discolour dissolve dwindle ebb melt away vanish

fail

(verb) If someone fails to achieve something, they are not successful.
e.g. *If I fail it is not the end of the world.*
be disappointed fall short flop founder misfire miss

failure

(noun) A failure is an unsuccessful person, thing, action, or event.
e.g. *The venture was a complete failure.*
collapse defeat disappointment fiasco flop incompetent loser loss washout wreck

faint

1. (adjective) Something that is faint has little strength or intensity.
e.g. *There was a faint smell of gas.*
dim faded feeble hazy indistinct low slight soft subdued vague weak

2. (verb) If you faint, you lose consciousness for a short time.
e.g. *Due to tiredness I often faint.*
black out collapse keel over pass out swoon

fair

(adjective) reasonable or equal according to generally accepted ideas about what is right and just.
e.g. *fair and prompt trials for political prisoners.*
disinterested dispassionate equal equitable honest impartial just objective unbiased

faith

(noun) Faith is a feeling of confidence, trust or optimism about something.
e.g. *I have little faith in the human race.*
confidence conviction reliance trust

faithful

(adjective) loyal to someone or something and remaining firm in support of them.
e.g. *a faithful friend.*
constant dependable devoted loyal reliable staunch steadfast true trusty

fake

1. (noun) A fake is an imitation of something made to trick people into thinking that it is genuine.
e.g. *a convincing fake of a 1930s radio.*
copy forgery fraud hoax imitation phoney reproduction sham

2. (adjective) Fake means imitation and not genuine.
e.g. *fake fur.*
bogus counterfeit false fraudulent imitation phoney reproduction sham

3. (verb) If you fake an emotion or feeling, you pretend that you are experiencing it.

e.g. *faking grief.*
counterfeit fabricate feign pretend put on simulate

false

1. (adjective) untrue, mistaken, or incorrect.
e.g. *The accusation is false and unjust.*
erroneous inaccurate incorrect mistaken unfounded wrong

2. not real or genuine but intended to seem real.
e.g. *false teeth.*
artificial bogus counterfeit fake imitation mock reproduction sham synthetic

fame

(noun) Fame is the state of being very well known.
e.g. *It is hard to find fame as a novelist.*
celebrity eminence glory prominence renown reputation stardom

familiar

1. (adjective) well known or easy to recognize.
e.g. *familiar faces.*
common customary everyday ordinary recognizable stock well known

2. knowing or understanding something well.
e.g. *Most children are familiar with the story of Cinderella.*
au fait conversant knowledgeable well up on

famous

(adjective) very well known.
e.g. *a famous actress.*
celebrated eminent honoured illustrious legendary notable noted prominent renowned

fan

(noun) If you are a fan of someone or something, you like them very much and are very enthusiastic about them.

e.g. *a football fan.*

enthusiast follower supporter

fanatic

(noun) A fanatic is a person who is very extreme in their support for a cause or in their enthusiasm for a particular sport or activity.

e.g. *a religious fanatic.*

addict bigot buff devotee diehard enthusiast extremist visionary zealot

fanatical

(adjective) If you are fanatical about something, you are very extreme in your enthusiasm or support for it.

e.g. *a fanatical patriot.*

bigoted burning extreme fervent frenzied immoderate obsessive overenthusiastic passionate rabid wild zealous

fancy

(adjective) Something that is fancy is special and elaborate.

e.g. *dressed up in some fancy clothes.*

elaborate elegant extravagant fanciful flowery intricate ornate

fantastic

(adjective) wonderful and very pleasing.

e.g. *a fantastic view of the sea.*

brilliant fabulous marvellous sensational stupendous superb wonderful

far

1. (adjective) Far means very distant.

e.g. *in the far south of England.*

deep distant outlying remote

2. (adverb) Far also means very much or to a great extent or

degree.

e.g. *far more important.*

considerably decidedly greatly incomparably much

far-fetched

(adjective) unlikely to be true.

e.g. *The theory is too far-fetched to be considered.*

doubtful dubious implausible improbable preposterous unconvincing unrealistic

fascinate

(verb) If something fascinates you, it interests and delights you so much that your thoughts concentrate on it and nothing else.

e.g. *a film that fascinates.*

absorb beguile bewitch captivate charm delight enchant engross enthral entrance intrigue

fashion

(noun) A fashion is a style of dress or way of behaving that is popular at a particular time.

e.g. *the fashion for tight clothing.*

craze fad latest mode rage style trend usage vogue

fashionable

(adjective) Something that is fashionable is very popular with a lot of people at the same time.

e.g. *the fashionable new drink.*

à la mode current in in vogue happening latest modern popular prevailing trendy up-to-date

fast

(adjective) moving, doing something, or happening quickly or with great speed.

e.g. *fast communications.*

brisk flying hasty hurried quick rapid speedy swift

fasten

(verb) To fasten something means to close it, do it up, or attach it firmly to something else.

e.g. *They were fastening a rope to a tree.*

affix attach bind bolt fix latch lock seal secure tie

fat

(adjective) Someone who is fat has too much weight on their body.

e.g. *a fat girl.*

corpulent gross heavy obese overweight plump podgy portly roly-poly rotund stout tubby

fatal

1. (adjective) very important or significant and likely to have an undesirable effect.

e.g. *The mistake was fatal to my plans.*

calamitous catastrophic disastrous ruinous

2. causing death.

e.g. *a fatal accident.*

deadly lethal malignant mortal terminal

fate

(noun) Fate is a power that is believed to control events.

e.g. *Fate was kind to Tara.*

chance destiny fortune predestination providence

fault

(noun) A fault in something or in someone's character is a weakness or imperfection in it.

e.g. *She was blind to his faults.*

blemish defect drawback failing flaw imperfection shortcoming weakness

faulty

(adjective) If something is faulty, it has something wrong with it.

e.g. *We traced the trouble to a faulty transformer.*
broken defective imperfect inaccurate malfunctioning out of order wrong

favourite

1. (adjective) Your favourite person or thing is the one you like best.
e.g. *She's one of my favourite writers.*
dearest favoured preferred

2. (noun) Someone's favourite is the person or thing they like best.
e.g. *Chocolate was his favourite.*
choice dear idol pet preference

favouritism

(noun) Favouritism is behaviour in which you are unfairly more helpful or more generous to one person than to other people.
e.g. *his favouritism towards his younger daughter.*
bias favour partiality preference prejudice

fear

(noun) Fear is an unpleasant feeling of danger.
e.g. *the fear of crime.*
alarm dread fright nightmare panic phobia terror trepidation

feather

(noun) A feather is one of the light fluffy structures covering a bird's body.
e.g. *ruffled ostrich feathers.*
plumage plume

feature

1. (noun) A feature of something is an interesting or important part or characteristic of it.
e.g. *Career guidance discussions were a feature of our final year.*

aspect facet factor point

2. A feature is an article or programme dealing with a particular subject.

e.g. *a feature on drug abuse.*

article column item piece report story

3. (verb) To feature something means to include it or emphasise it as being important.

e.g. *The film features two of my favourite actors.*

accentuate emphasise promote spotlight

feeble

(adjective) lacking power, strength, or influence.

e.g. *The management was feeble and cowardly.*

effete failing infirm powerless puny weak

feel

(verb) If you feel that something is the case, you believe it to be so.

e.g. *She feels that she is in control of her life.*

believe consider deem perceive sense think

feeling

(noun) Your feelings about something are your general attitudes, impressions, or thoughts about it.

e.g. *Americans have quite a different feeling about the press.*

idea impression instinct notion opinion perception view

fellowship

(noun) Fellowship is a feeling of friendliness that a group of people have when they are doing things together.

e.g. *Classes gathered together in fellowship.*

brotherhood camaraderie fraternity intimacy

fertile

(adjective) able to produce something easily or in large amounts.

e.g. *in the realm of her fertile imagination.*

flowering fruitful plentiful productive prolific rich teeming

festival

(noun) A festival is a day or period of religious celebration.
e.g. *a Buddhist festival.*
carnival celebration feast fiesta holiday

festive

(adjective) full of happiness and celebration.
e.g. *at Christmas or other festive occasions.*
celebratory convivial gala happy

feverish

(adjective) suffering from a high body temperature.
e.g. *a fevered brow.*
burning fevered flushed hot inflamed

fib

(noun) A fib is a small, unimportant lie.
e.g. *a fib about her exact age.*
lie prevarication story white lie

fidgety

(adjective) If you are fidgety, you keep changing your position because you are nervous or bored.
e.g. *The children are starting to get fidgety.*
impatient jittery jumpy nervous restive restless uneasy

field

(noun) A field is an area of land where crops are grown or animals are kept.
e.g. *We put the donkey in a field.*
grassland meadow pasture

fiendish

1. (adjective) very clever and imaginative.
e.g. *a fiendish plan.*
ingenious masterful

2. very difficult and challenging.
e.g. *fiendish mazes.*
daunting devilish diabolical tricky unspeakable wicked

fierce

(adjective) very aggressive or angry.
e.g. *a fierce personal attack.*
dangerous feral ferocious menacing savage threatening vicious violent

fight

1. (verb) When people fight, they take part in a battle, a war, a boxing match, or in some other attempt to hurt or kill someone.
e.g. *Riot police fought with crowds.*
brawl come to blows grapple scrap skirmish struggle tussle wrestle

2. (noun) A fight is a situation in which people hit or try to hurt each other.
e.g. *The man was killed in a fight.*
battle brawl conflict fracas free-for-all scrap scrimmage scuffle skirmish tussle

fill

(verb) If you fill something, it becomes full.
e.g. *a large hall filled with rows of desks.*
cram crowd pack pervade stock stuff swell

filth

(noun) Filth is disgusting dirt and muck.
e.g. *dust and filth on her skin.*
contamination dirt filthiness grime muck nastiness squalor

filthy

1. (adjective) Something that is filthy is disgustingly dirty.
e.g. *a really filthy oven.*
dirty foul grimy grubby mucky putrid squalid

2. morally unpleasant or disgusting, often about sexual matters.
e.g. *That's a filthy thing to say.*
coarse depraved dirty foul-mouthed impure indecent lewd obscene pornographic smutty suggestive

final

1. (adjective) last in a series or happening at the end of something.
e.g. *the final year of school.*
closing concluding last terminating ultimate

2. Something that is final cannot be changed or questioned.
e.g. *The judges' decision is final.*
absolute conclusive definite definitive incontrovertible irrevocable settled

finale

(noun) The finale is the last section of a piece of music or show.
e.g. *the finale of Shostakovich's Fifth Symphony.*
climax close conclusion culmination

finally

1. (adverb) If something finally happens, it happens after a long delay.
e.g. *She finally left her room.*
at last at length eventually in the end ultimately

2. You use the word finally to introduce a final point, question, or topic that you are talking or writing about.
e.g. *Finally, a word about the New Forest.*
in conclusion in summary lastly to conclude

financial

(adjective) relating to or involving money.

e.g. *financial problems.*

economic fiscal monetary money pecuniary

find

(verb) If you find someone or something, you discover them, either as a result of searching or by coming across them unexpectedly.

e.g. *I need to find a job.*

come across discover encounter espy locate meet recognize spot unearth

finish

1. (verb) When you finish something, you reach the end of it and complete it.

e.g. *I've finished my project.*

complete conclude discharge end execute fulfil wind up wrap up

2. When something finishes, it ends or stops.

e.g. *The conversation finished.*

cease close conclude stop terminate

3. (noun) The finish of something is the end or last part of it.

e.g. *from the start of his career to the finish.*

cessation close completion conclusion ending

fire

1. (noun) Fire is the flames produced when something burns.

e.g. *damage by fire.*

blaze flames

2. A fire is a pile or mass of burning material.

e.g. *a house fire.*

conflagration inferno

firm

1. (adjective) Something that is firm does not move if it is pushed or shaken.

e.g. *Bake the cake for about an hour till the surface is risen and firm.*

compact congealed fixed hard inelastic secure solid stable tight unshakable

2. Something that is firm is definite and unlikely to change.

e.g. *They want a firm decision by next Monday.*

definite fixed inflexible resolute strict unyielding

first

(adjective) happening, coming, or done before everything or everyone else.

e.g. *That's the first thing to remember.*

chief earliest foremost fundamental key leading opening original pre-eminent primary principal

fit

1. (verb) If something fits a particular situation, person, or thing, it is suitable or appropriate.

e.g. *a sentence that fitted the crime.*

accord with correspond go match meet suit

2. (noun) If someone has a fit, their muscles suddenly start contracting violently and they may lose consciousness.

e.g. *He had an inexplicable fit.*

convulsion paroxysm seizure spasm

fix

(verb) If you fix something broken, you mend it.

e.g. *He fixed the door.*

mend repair secure

flabby

(adjective) Someone who is flabby is rather fat and unfit, with loose flesh on their body.

e.g. *She was plump and rather flabby.*

flaccid out of condition sagging slack unfit

flag

(noun) A flag is a rectangle or square of cloth of a particular colour and design which is used as the symbol of a nation, or as a signal.

e.g. *the British flag.*

banner ensign pennant standard

flashy

(adjective) expensive and fashionable in a rather vulgar way.

e.g. *a flashy car.*

flamboyant garish gaudy jazzy *informal* loud ostentatious showy tasteless

flat

(adjective) Something that is flat is level and smooth.

e.g. *a bit of flat land.*

even horizontal level unbroken

flatter

(verb) If you flatter someone, you praise them in an exaggerated way, either to please them or to persuade them to do something.

e.g. *I knew she was just flattering me.*

butter up cajole fawn sweet-talk

flattery

(noun) Flattery is flattering words or behaviour.

e.g. *Blatant flattery will embarrass.*

blandishment blarney fawning obsequiousness sweet-talk

flaw

1. (noun) A flaw is a fault or mark in a piece of fabric, china, or glass, or in a decorative pattern.

e.g. *a flaw in a stone.*

blemish imperfection mark speck spot

2. A flaw is also a weak point or undesirable quality in a theory, plan, or person's character.
e.g. *the flaw in my argument.*
blemish defect failing fault imperfection weakness

fleck

(noun) A fleck is a small coloured mark or particle.
e.g. *a fleck of paint.*
speck speckle spot

flexible

1. (adjective) able to be bent easily without breaking.
e.g. *The tube is flexible but tough.*
elastic pliable pliant springy

2. able to adapt to changing circumstances.
e.g. *a flexible arrangement.*
adaptable adjustable discretionary open variable

flight

(noun) Flight is the action of flying or the ability to fly.
e.g. *the mysteries of flight.*
aviation flying

flinch

(verb) If you flinch, you make a sudden small movement in fear or pain.
e.g. *She flinched at the noise.*
blench cringe duck quail recoil shrink start wince

flirt

(verb) If you flirt with an idea, you consider it without seriously intending to do anything about it.
e.g. *I flirted with the idea of becoming a gambler.*
dally play toy

flood

1. (noun) A flood is a large amount of water covering an area that is usually dry.

e.g. *a huge flood of rain.*

deluge downpour flash flood inundation spate torrent

2. A flood of something is a large amount of it suddenly occurring.

e.g. *a flood of angry language.*

glut profusion rush spate stream surge swarm tide

floppy

(adjective) tending to hang downwards in a rather loose way.

e.g. *a floppy, outsize jacket.*

droopy flaccid limp sagging slack

fluent

(adjective) able to express yourself clearly and without hesitation.

e.g. *fluent in several languages.*

articulate eloquent flowing voluble

fly

(verb) When a bird, insect, or aircraft flies, it moves through the air.

e.g. *A small hawk flies near.*

flit flutter glide sail soar

foam

(noun) Foam is a mass of tiny bubbles.

e.g. *the white foam at the water's edge.*

bubbles froth lather spray spume suds

foible

(noun) A foible is a minor eccentricity in a person's character.

e.g. *all sorts of human foibles.*

eccentricity idiosyncrasy oddity peculiarity quirk

foil

(verb) If you foil someone's attempt at something, you prevent them from succeeding.

e.g. *Their attempt to recapture Calais was foiled by a traitor.*

balk check circumvent defeat frustrate nullify thwart

fold

(verb) If you fold something, you bend it so that one part lies over another.

e.g. *He folded his napkin.*

crease double over layer overlap pleat tuck

follow

(verb) Something that follows a particular thing happens after it.

e.g. *Night follows day.*

ensue succeed

follower

(noun) The followers of a person or belief are the people who support them.

e.g. *a follower of Christ.*

adherent admirer believer devotee disciple fan supporter

folly

(noun) Folly is a foolish act or foolish behaviour.

e.g. *the extremes of human folly.*

absurdity foolishness idiocy imprudence indiscretion irrationality lunacy madness nonsense recklessness stupidity

fond

(adjective) If you are fond of someone or something, you like them.

e.g. *We are still very fond of each other.*

adoring affectionate attached caring devoted doting

indulgent loving tender

food

(noun) Food is any substance consumed by an animal or plant to provide energy.

e.g. *daily food supplies.*

fare foodstuff nourishment provisions rations sustenance victuals

fool

(noun) Someone who is a fool behaves in a silly way.

e.g. *She was not fool enough to think it would be easy.*

ass clot *informal* dunce dunderhead halfwit idiot ignoramus nincompoop simpleton twerp *informal* twit *informal*

foolish

(adjective) very silly or unwise.

e.g. *foolish risks.*

absurd asinine harebrained idiotic ill-advised imprudent inane indiscreet injudicious ridiculous senseless short-sighted silly unreasonable unwise

force

(verb) To force someone to do something means to make them do it.

e.g. *Don't force me to cook.*

bind coerce compel constrain dragoon drive impel make oblige pressurize

forced

(adjective) Something that is forced is done with an effort and is not natural or spontaneous.

e.g. *a forced smile.*

artificial contrived false insincere laboured stiff strained unnatural wooden

foreign

(adjective) unfamiliar or uncharacteristic.

e.g. *Such daft enthusiasm was foreign to him.*

alien outlandish strange unfamiliar unknown

forgive

(verb) If you forgive someone for doing something bad, you stop feeling angry and resentful towards them.

e.g. *He forgave her for past injuries.*

absolve excuse exonerate pardon

formidable

(adjective) very difficult to deal with or overcome, and therefore rather frightening or impressive.

e.g. *formidable enemies.*

challenging colossal daunting difficult intimidating onerous overwhelming

fort

(noun) A fort is a strong building built for defence.

e.g. *a fort overlooking the harbour.*

citadel fortress garrison stronghold

forte

(noun) If something is your forte, you are particularly good at doing it.

e.g. *Languages have never been your forte.*

métier speciality strength strong point

fragile

(adjective) easily broken or damaged.

e.g. *a fragile ornament.*

breakable brittle delicate flimsy frail weak

fragrance

(noun) A fragrance is a sweet or pleasant smell.

e.g. *the fragrance of flowers.*

aroma bouquet perfume scent smell

frank

(adjective) If you are frank, you say things in an open and honest way.

e.g. *a frank confession.*

blunt candid direct downright forthright open outright outspoken plain sincere straightforward

free

1. (adjective) Someone who is free is no longer a prisoner.

e.g. *Three innocent men are free after years in prison.*

at large at liberty liberated on the loose

2. If something is free, you can have it without paying for it.

e.g. *free drinks.*

complimentary gratis on the house

3. (verb) If you free something that is fastened or trapped, you release it.

e.g. *a campaign to free captive animals.*

extricate loose release set free turn loose unleash untie

4. When a prisoner is freed, he or she is released.

e.g. *Armed men freed her from prison.*

discharge emancipate liberate release

freedom

1. (noun) If you have the freedom to do something, you have the scope or are allowed to do it.

e.g. *freedom of speech.*

carte blanche *French* discretion facility flexibility latitude leeway licence opportunity power scope

2. When prisoners gain their freedom, they escape or are released.

e.g. *her third day of freedom from prison.*

emancipation liberty release

frenzy

(noun) If someone is in a frenzy, their behaviour is wild and uncontrolled.

e.g. *a drunken frenzy.*

agitation fever fit fury outburst paroxysm passion

friend

(noun) Your friends are people you know well and like to spend time with.

e.g. *She and Hannah had been friends for years.*

chum companion comrade confidant crony pal

friendly

(adjective) If you are friendly to someone, you behave in a kind and pleasant way to them.

e.g. *The staff are experienced, friendly and helpful.*

affable amiable amicable close companionable convivial cordial genial intimate sociable sympathetic welcoming well-disposed

friendship

(noun) Friendship is the state of being friends with someone.

e.g. *I shared a warm friendship with Felicity.*

amity camaraderie closeness friendliness intimacy rapport

frighten

(verb) If something frightens you, it makes you afraid.

e.g. *The situation was beginning to frighten me.*

alarm dismay intimidate petrify scare shock startle terrify unnerve

frivolous

(adjective) Someone who is frivolous behaves in a silly or light-hearted way, especially when they should be serious or sensible.

e.g. *his outwardly frivolous attitude.*

childish empty-headed flighty flippant juvenile puerile silly superficial

frolic

(verb) When animals or children frolic, they run around and play in a lively way.

e.g. *Puppies frolic happily on the lawn.*

caper cavort frisk gambol play prance romp

frozen

(adjective) If you are frozen, you are extremely cold.

e.g. *Savage was tired and frozen.*

chilled frigid ice-cold icy numb

frugal

1. (adjective) Someone who is frugal spends very little money.

e.g. *Mary is severely frugal with herself.*

abstemious careful economical parsimonious prudent saving sparing thrifty

2. A frugal meal is small and cheap.

e.g. *I had our frugal breakfast ready.*

insubstantial meagre niggardly

frustrate

(verb) To frustrate something such as a plan means to prevent it.

e.g. *She hopes to frustrate the engagement of her son.*

balk block defeat foil forestall stymie thwart

full

(adjective) containing or having as much as it is possible to hold.

e.g. *His room is full of posters.*

brimful chock-a-block chock-full crammed crowded filled gorged jammed loaded packed replete sated stocked

fun

(noun) Fun is enjoyable lighthearted activity or amusement.
e.g. *That would have spoiled the fun.*
amusement diversion enjoyment entertainment gaiety jollity merrymaking pleasure recreation sport

fund

(verb) Someone who funds something provides money for it.
e.g. *research funded by pharmaceutical companies.*
endow finance float promote sponsor subsidize support

funny

1. (adjective) strange or puzzling.
e.g. *It's funny that you met the same people.*
curious mysterious odd peculiar perplexing puzzling queer remarkable rum strange suspicious unusual weird

2. causing amusement or laughter.
e.g. *a funny old film.*
amusing comic comical diverting droll entertaining farcical hilarious humorous jocular witty

furniture

(noun) Furniture is movable objects such as tables, chairs and wardrobes.
e.g. *17th century oak furniture.*
effects fittings furnishings

further

(verb) If you further something, you help it to progress.
e.g. *This success will certainly further your career.*
advance assist champion expedite foster promote

fuss

(noun) Fuss is unnecessarily anxious or excited behaviour.
e.g. *They played with no fuss in the playroom.*
ado agitation bother bustle commotion confusion

excitement flurry fluster palaver to-do trouble

fussy

(adjective) likely to fuss a lot.

e.g. *He was unusually fussy about keeping things perfect.*

choosy exacting faddy fastidious finicky particular pernickety *informal*

futile

(adjective) having no chance of success.

e.g. *a futile attempt to calm the storm.*

abortive fruitless pointless to no avail unavailing unproductive unprofitable unsuccessful useless vain

G g

gadget

(noun) A gadget is a small machine or tool.

e.g. *a new gadget that makes driving safer.*

appliance contraption *informal* device tool

gamble

1. (verb) When people gamble, they bet money or play games like roulette in order to try and win money.

e.g. *Many workers gamble on horses and greyhounds.*

bet wager

2. If you gamble something, you risk losing it in the hope of gaining an advantage.

e.g. *The company gambled everything on the new factory.*

chance hazard risk stake

game

(noun) A game is an enjoyable activity with a set of rules which is played by individuals or teams against each other.

e.g. *I spent the day reading and playing games.*

diversion pastime play recreation sport

gap

(noun) A gap is a space between two things or a hole in something solid.

e.g. *They squeezed through a gap in the fence.*

breach break chink cleft crack divide hole opening space

garbled

(adjective) Garbled messages are jumbled and the details may be

wrong.
e.g. *her garbled version of events.*
confused distorted

gather

1. (verb) When people gather, they come together in a group.
e.g. *Hundreds of people gathered at the scene.*
assemble collect congregate convene flock group

2. If you gather a number of things, you collect them or bring them together in one place.
e.g. *He gathered up the rubbish and put it in a bag.*
amass assemble collect group marshal muster round up

gaudy

(adjective) very colourful in a vulgar way.
e.g. *gaudy T-shirts.*
bright flamboyant garish loud

gauzy

(adjective) light, thin, and almost transparent.
e.g. *She was wearing a robe of some gauzy, shimmering material.*
diaphanous filmy sheer wispy

general

1. (adjective) relating to the whole of something or to most things in a group, rather than to separate parts.
e.g. *your general health.*
broad overall

2. true, suitable, or relevant in most situations.
e.g. *the general opinion.*
common extensive overall popular prevailing prevalent universal widespread

generous

1. (adjective) A generous person is very willing to give money,

time, or gifts.

e.g. *Mrs Zuckerman is very generous with advice and information.*

free lavish liberal munificent open-handed

2. Something that is generous is very large.

e.g. *a generous helping of pudding.*

abundant bountiful lavish liberal

get

1. (verb) 'Get' often means the same as 'become'.

e.g. *She began to get suspicious.*

become grow turn

2. If you get something, you fetch it, receive it, or are given it.

e.g. *Get me a glass of water.*

acquire bring come by fetch obtain procure secure

get at

1. (verb) If someone is getting at you, they are criticizing you in an unkind way.

e.g. *He's been getting at me all day.*

attack criticize find fault with pick on

2. If you ask someone what they are getting at, you are asking them to explain what they mean.

e.g. *I can't imagine what you're getting at.*

hint imply mean suggest

ghost

(noun) A ghost is the spirit of a dead person, believed to haunt people or places.

e.g. *It is said that his ghost still roams the grounds of the castle.*

phantom soul spectre spirit spook *informal* wraith

give

(verb) If you give someone something, you hand it to them or provide it for them.

e.g. *I gave him some money.*

bestow confer furnish grant impart present provide supply

give in

(verb) If you give in, you admit that you are defeated.

e.g. *We argued for a while, but eventually I gave in.*

admit defeat submit surrender yield

glib

(adjective) speaking or spoken quickly and confidently but without sincerity.

e.g. *a glib reply.*

quick ready slick smooth smooth-tongued

gloss

(noun) Gloss is a bright shine on a surface.

e.g. *This polish gives a wonderful gloss to wood.*

lustre sheen shine

glossy

(adjective) smooth and shiny.

e.g. *glossy hair.*

lustrous shining shiny sleek smooth

glower

(verb) If you glower, you stare angrily.

e.g. *They glowered at each other across the table.*

frown glare scowl

go

1. (verb) If you go, you move or travel from one place to get to another.

e.g. *I wasn't going to go until he arrived.*

depart journey leave set off travel withdraw

2. If something goes well, it is successful. If it goes badly, it is unsuccessful.

e.g. *All will go well as long as you trust your intuition.*
fare happen proceed result turn out work out

3. If a machine or clock goes, it works and is not broken.
e.g. *This clock goes for months on one little battery.*
function operate perform run work

4. (noun) A go is an attempt at doing something.
e.g. *Isn't it fun having a go at a foreign language?*
attempt crack *informal* shot *informal* stab *informal* try turn whack *informal*

go on

1. (verb) If you go on doing something, you continue to do it.
e.g. *I couldn't go on living with him.*
carry on continue keep on persist proceed

2. Something that is going on is happening.
e.g. *We looked out to see what was going on.*
happen occur

go through

(verb) If you go through an unpleasant event, you experience it.
e.g. *I wouldn't go through that again for all the tea in China.*
bear endure experience suffer tolerate undergo

gobble

(verb) If you gobble food, you eat it very quickly.
e.g. *He gobbled all the beef stew.*
bolt devour gorge guzzle scoff wolf

good

1. (adjective) pleasant, acceptable, or satisfactory.
e.g. *a good night's sleep.*
acceptable excellent fine first-class first-rate great pleasant satisfactory splendid super *informal*

2. skilful or successful.
e.g. *a good goalscorer.*

able accomplished adept capable competent efficient expert proficient skilled talented

3. well-behaved.
e.g. *He was a good boy when he was young.*
mannerly obedient polite well-behaved well-mannered

4. (noun) Good is moral and spiritual justice and rightness.
e.g. *the eternal struggle between good and evil.*
goodness morality right righteousness virtue

5. Good also refers to anything that is desirable, useful, or beneficial as opposed to harmful.
e.g. *It is a decision she has made for the good of the company.*
advantage benefit gain profit welfare well-being

goodbye

(interjection) You say 'Goodbye' when you are leaving someone or ending a telephone conversation.
e.g. *I said goodbye and walked away.*
adieu cheerio *informal* farewell

grab

1. (verb) If you grab something, you take it or pick it up roughly.
e.g. *She grabbed the suitcase.*
clutch grasp grip seize snatch

2. If you grab an opportunity, you take advantage of it eagerly.
e.g. *He grabbed the chance to launch a blistering attack.*
grasp seize snatch

grace

(noun) Grace is an elegant way of moving.
e.g. *She walked with grace.*
charm elegance gracefulness poise

grain

1. (noun) A grain of sand or salt is a tiny particle of it.

e.g. *A single grain of sand can wreck a camcorder's tape deck.*
granule particle speck

2. A grain of a quality is a tiny amount of it.
e.g. *There was a grain of truth in his story.*
iota particle speck

grand

(adjective) magnificent in appearance and size.
e.g. *a grand palace.*
august fine great imposing impressive lofty magnificent majestic noble opulent princely regal splendid stately striking

grateful

(adjective) If you are grateful for something, you are glad you have it and want to thank the person who gave it to you.
e.g. *We are grateful for their support.*
appreciative indebted obliged thankful

gratitude

(noun) Gratitude is the feeling of being grateful.
e.g. *I wish to express my gratitude to Kathy.*
appreciation gratefulness indebtedness thankfulness thanks

greedy

(adjective) wanting more of something, such as food, than you really need.
e.g. *I'm very greedy and can't resist second helpings.*
acquisitive avaricious gluttonous grasping insatiable piggish rapacious selfish voracious

greet

(verb) If you greet someone, you say something friendly like 'hello' to them when you meet them.
e.g. *Charlie came bounding out to greet her.*
hail salute

grief

(noun) Grief is extreme sadness.

e.g. *her grief over her mother's death.*

heartache heartbreak misery sadness sorrow woe

grieve

(verb) If you grieve, you are extremely sad, especially because someone has died.

e.g. *Families grieved for the loss of their loved ones.*

bemoan bewail lament mourn sorrow

grind

(verb) If you grind something such as corn or pepper, you crush it into a fine powder.

e.g. *He's got one of those machines that grinds coffee beans.*

crush mill pound powder pulverize

groove

(noun) A groove is a deep line cut into a surface.

e.g. *a groove sliced into the wood.*

channel furrow hollow rut score

group

(noun) A group of things or people is a number of them that are linked together in some way.

e.g. *a small group of friends.*

assembly band bevy bunch category class collection crowd gang gathering party

grow

(verb) To grow means to increase in size, amount, or degree.

e.g. *The company has grown from a one-man business to a multinational corporation in only ten years.*

develop enlarge expand extend increase multiply rise

spread swell wax widen

growth

(noun) When there is a growth in something, it gets bigger.

e.g. *the growth in political opposition.*

development enlargement expansion extension growing increase increment rise

gruelling

(adjective) difficult and tiring.

e.g. *a gruelling race.*

arduous demanding difficult exhausting fierce grinding hard harsh laborious punishing severe stiff strenuous taxing tiring trying

grumpy

(adjective) bad-tempered and fed-up.

e.g. *a grumpy old man.*

bad-tempered gruff ill-tempered irascible irritable snappy surly testy touchy

guarantee

1. (verb) If something or someone guarantees something, they make it certain that it will happen.

e.g. *Freedom does not guarantee happiness.*

assure ensure promise secure warrant

2. (noun) If something is a guarantee of something else, it makes it certain that it will happen.

e.g. *a guarantee of safety.*

assurance pledge promise security warranty

guard

1. (verb) If you guard a person or object, you stay near to them either to protect them or to make sure they do not escape.

e.g. *Sentries guarded the gates.*

cover defend escort mind patrol protect safeguard shield

2. (noun) A guard is a person or group of people who guard a person, object, or place.

e.g. *Two guards were stationed at the main entrance.*

escort lookout patrol protector sentinel sentry warden warder watchman

guess

1. (verb) If you guess something, you form or express an opinion that it is the case, without having much information.

e.g. *He guessed the answer.*

conjecture estimate speculate suppose surmise

2. (noun) A guess is an attempt to give the correct answer to something without having much information.

e.g. *Have a guess what the time is.*

conjecture speculation supposition theory

gullible

(adjective) easily tricked.

e.g. *Hunt had already fooled four gullible women.*

credulous foolish green innocent naive trusting unsuspecting

gush

1. (verb) When liquid gushes from something, it flows out of it in large quantities.

e.g. *Rain gushed down the hillsides.*

burst cascade flood flow jet pour run rush spout spurt stream

2. When people gush, they express admiration or pleasure in an exaggerated way.

e.g. *Agents gushed about the discovery.*

effuse enthuse

guts

(plural noun) Your guts are your internal organs, especially your

intestines.
e.g. *I felt a pain in my guts.*
bowels entrails innards intestines

H h

hackneyed

(adjective) A hackneyed phrase is meaningless because it has been used too often.

e.g. *hackneyed dialogue.*

clichéd overworked stock

hamper

(verb) If you hamper someone, you make it difficult for them to move or progress.

e.g. *He has been hampered by injuries.*

encumber fetter handicap hinder hold up impede limit restrict retard

handicap

(noun) A handicap is a physical or mental disability.

e.g. *John was born with the handicap of having no proper arms.*

disability impairment impediment

handsome

(adjective) very attractive in appearance.

e.g. *a handsome young actor.*

attractive comely good-looking

hang

(verb) If you hang something somewhere, you attach it to a high point. If it is hanging there, it is attached by its top to something.

e.g. *His jacket hung from a hook behind the door.*

dangle drape suspend

happen

(verb) When something happens, it occurs or takes place.

e.g. *The accident happened at midnight.*

befall come about occur transpire

happy

(adjective) feeling, showing, or producing contentment or pleasure.

e.g. *a happy smile.*

blissful blithe cheerful content contented glad jolly joyful merry pleased

hard

1. (adjective) Something that is hard is firm, solid, or stiff.

e.g. *a hard piece of cheese.*

firm rigid set solid stiff tough

2. requiring a lot of effort.

e.g. *hard work.*

arduous exacting exhausting laborious rigorous strenuous tough uphill

3. difficult.

e.g. *a hard problem.*

baffling complex complicated difficult intricate involved perplexing puzzling thorny

harm

(verb) To harm someone or something means to injure or damage them.

e.g. *He did not intend to harm the child.*

damage hurt ill-treat injure maltreat wound

harsh

(adjective) severe, difficult, and unpleasant.

e.g. *harsh criticism.*

cruel grim hard severe tough unpleasant

hate

(verb) If you hate someone or something, you have a strong dislike for them.

e.g. *He hates driving in London.*

abhor abominate despise detest dislike loathe

hateful

(adjective) extremely unpleasant.

e.g. *Robert had just come from a hateful school.*

abhorrent abominable despicable detestable horrible loathsome obnoxious odious

haughty

(adjective) showing excessive pride.

e.g. *He behaved in a haughty manner.*

arrogant disdainful high and mighty lofty proud snobbish snooty *informal* supercilious

health

(noun) Health is the normally good condition of someone's body and the extent to which it is free from illness.

e.g. *Vitamins are essential for health.*

fitness healthiness soundness wellbeing

healthy

(adjective) Someone who is healthy is fit and strong and does not have any diseases.

e.g. *Healthy people rarely seek out a doctor.*

fit hale hardy robust sound strong well

heap

(noun) A heap of things is a pile of them.

e.g. *a heap of scrap metal.*

lot mass mound mountain pile stack

hear

(verb) When you hear sounds, you are aware of them because they reach your ears.

e.g. *He heard the noise of a radio from another room.*

catch listen to overhear perceive

heed

(verb) If you heed someone's advice, you pay attention to it.

e.g. *Harry refused to heed the warning.*

mark mind note

help

1. (verb) To help someone means to make something easier, better, or quicker for them.

e.g. *I helped him with his homework.*

aid assist oblige support

2. (noun) If you need or give help, you need or give assistance.

e.g. *He wants some help with a bit of building work.*

aid assistance succour support

3. A help is someone or something that helps you.

e.g. *He really is a good help.*

aid assistance benefit support

helpful

(adjective) If someone is helpful, they help you by doing something for you.

e.g. *Martin found the nurses extremely helpful.*

accommodating cooperative kind obliging supportive useful

hesitant

(adjective) If you are hesitant, you do not do something immediately because you are uncertain, worried, or embarrassed.

e.g. *I was a little hesitant about approaching too closely.*

doubtful indecisive irresolute uncertain unsure vacillating wavering

hesitate

(verb) To hesitate means to pause or show uncertainty.

e.g. *She hesitated before replying.*

dither falter pause vacillate waver

hide

(verb) To hide something means to put it where it cannot be seen, or to prevent it from being discovered.

e.g. *He was unable to hide his disappointment.*

bury cloak conceal cover mask obscure screen secrete stash veil

high

1. (adjective) tall or a long way above the ground.

e.g. *a high wall.*

elevated lofty soaring steep tall towering

2. (adverb) at or to a height.

e.g. *The flag flew high on the main tower.*

aloft

hike

1. (noun) A hike is a long country walk.

e.g. *a fifteen-mile hike.*

march ramble tramp trek walk

2. (verb) To hike means to walk long distances in the country.

e.g. *I hiked to the summit.*

march ramble tramp trek walk

hilarious

(adjective) very funny.

e.g. *There are some really hilarious moments in this film.*

amusing comical funny humorous hysterical side-splitting uproarious

hint

1. (noun) A hint is a suggestion or clue about something.

e.g. *There was no hint of any foul play.*

clue implication indication insinuation intimation suggestion

2. A hint is also a helpful piece of advice.

e.g. *some useful hints to help them improve their ratings.*

advice pointer tip

3. (verb) If you hint at something, you suggest it indirectly.

e.g. *He liked to hint at deep secrets.*

allude imply insinuate intimate suggest

hire

(verb) If you hire something, you pay money to be able to use it for a period of time.

e.g. *Occasionally, I will hire a video.*

charter engage lease rent

hit

(verb) To hit someone or something means to strike or touch them forcefully, usually causing hurt or damage.

e.g. *The car hit a tree.*

bang bash *informal* knock smack strike thump wallop *informal* whack

hoard

1. (verb) To hoard things means to save them even though they may no longer be useful.

e.g. *Helen had hoarded discarded woollens.*

collect gather save stash stockpile store treasure

2. (noun) A hoard is a store of things that has been saved or hidden.

e.g. *a hoard of treasure.*

cache reserve stash stockpile store supply

hoarse

(adjective) A hoarse voice sounds rough and unclear.

e.g. *a hoarse whisper.*

croaky gravelly gruff harsh husky rasping rough

hold

1. (verb) To hold something means to carry, support, or keep it in place, usually with your hand or arms.

e.g. *I held the baby in my arms.*

clasp cling clutch cradle grasp grip

2. If you hold something such as a meeting, a party, or an election, you arrange it and cause it to happen.

e.g. *Mr Mason held a party to celebrate.*

arrange conduct convene have run

hold off

(verb) To hold something off means to prevent or delay it.

e.g. *We held off from testing the boat last year.*

defer delay postpone prevent put off

hold out

(verb) If you hold out, you stand firm and manage to resist opposition in difficult circumstances.

e.g. *The rebels could hold out for ten years.*

carry on continue endure hang on last stand fast

hold up

(verb) If something holds you up, it delays you.

e.g. *The traffic was held up by a procession.*

delay detain hinder slow down

hole

(noun) A hole is an opening or hollow in something.

e.g. *a hole in the wall.*

aperture cavity gap hollow opening

holy

1. (adjective) relating to God or to a particular religion.

e.g. *the holy city.*

divine hallowed religious sacred

2. Someone who is holy is religious and leads a pure and good life.

e.g. *a very holy lady.*

devout godly pious pure religious righteous saintly virtuous

home

(noun) Your home is the building, place, or country in which you live or feel you belong.

e.g. *his home in Oxford.*

abode dwelling house pad *slang* residence

homely

(adjective) simple, ordinary and comfortable.

e.g. *The room was small and homely.*

comfortable cosy snug

honest

(adjective) truthful and trustworthy.

e.g. *honest friends and neighbours.*

above board genuine honourable straight trustworthy truthful upright veracious

honesty

(noun) Honesty is the quality of being truthful and trustworthy.

e.g. *His honesty earned him a high reputation.*

honour integrity trustworthiness truthfulness

honorary

(adjective) An honorary title or job is given as a mark of respect or honour, and does not involve the usual qualifications, work, or payment.

e.g. *She was awarded an honorary degree.*
complimentary nominal titular

hooligan

(noun) A hooligan is a noisy, destructive, and violent young person.
e.g. *German courts are cracking down on hooligans.*
delinquent lout ruffian vandal

horrible

(adjective) causing shock, fear, or disgust.
e.g. *The Inspector had seen many horrible crimes.*
appalling awful dreadful frightful ghastly grim gruesome hideous horrendous horrid horrific repulsive revolting shocking terrible

hug

1. (verb) If you hug someone, you put your arms round them and hold them close to you.
e.g. *He wanted to pick up his child and hug her.*
clasp cuddle embrace enfold

2. (noun) If you give someone a hug, you hold them close to you.
e.g. *She greeted me with a hug and kiss.*
cuddle embrace

huge

(adjective) extremely large in amount, size, or degree.
e.g. *a huge success.*
colossal enormous gargantuan giant gigantic great immense large mammoth massive tremendous vast

humble

1. (adjective) A humble person is modest and thinks that he or she has very little value.
e.g. *Andy was a humble and gentle man.*

lowly modest unassuming

2. Something that is humble is small or not very important.
e.g. *Just a splash of wine will transform a humble casserole.*
insignificant modest ordinary simple unimportant

humid

(adjective) If it is humid, the air feels damp, heavy, and warm.
e.g. *Visitors can expect hot and humid conditions.*
clammy damp moist muggy steamy sticky sultry

humiliate

(verb) To humiliate someone means to make them feel ashamed or appear stupid to other people.
e.g. *He set out to injure and humiliate victims.*
disgrace embarrass humble mortify shame

humour

(noun) Humour is the quality of being funny.
e.g. *They discussed it with tact and humour.*
amusement comedy fun wit

hungry

(adjective) needing or wanting to eat.
e.g. *My friends went to bed hungry.*
empty famished peckish *informal* ravenous starved starving

hurry

1. (verb) To hurry means to move or do something as quickly as possible.
e.g. *She hurried through the empty streets.*
dash fly hasten rush scurry

2. (noun) Hurry is the speed with which you do something quickly.
e.g. *He was in a hurry to leave.*

haste quickness rush speed urgency

hygiene

(noun) Hygiene is the practice of keeping yourself and your surroundings clean, especially in order to prevent the spread of disease.

e.g. *high standards of hygiene.*

cleanliness sanitation

hypnotize

(verb) To hypnotize someone means to put them into a state in which they seem to be asleep but can respond to questions and suggestions.

e.g. *Patients are hypnotized and encouraged to remember their past lives.*

entrance mesmerize

hysterical

(adjective) Someone who is hysterical is in a state of uncontrolled excitement, anger, or panic.

e.g. *Sharon was almost hysterical with anxiety.*

beside yourself frantic frenzied mad overwrought uncontrollable

I i

idea

1. (noun) An idea is a plan, suggestion, or thought that you have after thinking about a problem.

e.g. *an idea for starting a business.*

feeling hunch impression inkling notion thought

2. An idea is also an opinion or belief.

e.g. *We've all got very different ideas about music.*

belief concept image interpretation notion opinion perception thought understanding view viewpoint

idiot

(noun) If you call someone an idiot, you mean that they are stupid or foolish.

e.g. *He was an idiot to believe that he would win.*

ass fool halfwit imbecile moron *informal* nincompoop nitwit *informal* simpleton twit *informal*

idiotic

(adjective) extremely foolish or silly.

e.g. *idiotic behaviour.*

asinine crass crazy dim fatuous foolish halfwitted inane senseless stupid

ignorant

(adjective) If you are ignorant of something, you do not know about it.

e.g. *He seems totally ignorant of the rules of cricket.*

green *informal* inexperienced innocent oblivious unaware unconscious

ill

(adjective) unhealthy or sick.

e.g. *He became ill with stomach ulcers.*

ailing indisposed off-colour poorly queasy queer sick under the weather *informal* unhealthy unwell

illegal

(adjective) forbidden by the law.

e.g. *illegal betting.*

criminal illicit lawless unauthorized unconstitutional unlawful

illness

(noun) An illness is a particular disease.

e.g. *childhood illnesses such as measles, mumps, and whooping cough.*

ailment complaint disease disorder indisposition malady sickness

imagine

1. (verb) If you imagine something, you form an idea of it in your mind, or you think you have seen or heard it but you have not really.

e.g. *I just imagined I was in France or Germany.*

conceive conjure up envisage picture visualize

2. If you imagine that something is the case, you believe it is the case.

e.g. *I imagine he has a lot of sleep to catch up on.*

fancy think

imitate

(verb) To imitate someone or something means to copy them.

e.g. *Benedict could imitate Israeli accents.*

ape copy echo emulate follow impersonate mimic mirror simulate

imminent

(adjective) If something is imminent, it is going to happen very soon.

e.g. *Police said more arrests were imminent.*

forthcoming impending in the offing looming prospective

impartial

(adjective) Someone who is impartial has a fair and unbiased view of something.

e.g. *Scientists can be expected to be impartial.*

detached disinterested equitable fair just neutral objective open-minded

imperfect

(adjective) Something that is imperfect has faults or problems.

e.g. *an imperfect system.*

damaged defective faulty flawed impaired incomplete limited

impersonal

(adjective) An impersonal feeling or action does not relate to any particular person.

e.g. *impersonal criticism of the firm.*

clinical cold detached dispassionate formal inhuman neutral remote

important

(adjective) Something that is important is very valuable, necessary, or significant.

e.g. *important new medical developments.*

eminent foremost grave great high influential leading momentous portentous prominent salient serious significant substantial urgent weighty

impose

(verb) If you impose something on people, you force it on them.

e.g. *The allies had imposed a ban on all flights over Iraq.*

enforce establish foist inflict introduce lay levy

impression

1. (noun) An impression of someone or something is the way they seem to you.

e.g. *They give the impression of not working.*

effect feeling idea impact sense

2. An impression of an object is a mark or shape that it has left in something soft.

e.g. *the mark left by the impression of the shoe.*

imprint stamp

impressionable

(adjective) easy to influence.

e.g. *impressionable teenagers.*

receptive responsive suggestible susceptible vulnerable

improbable

(adjective) not probable or likely to happen.

e.g. *an improbable tale.*

doubtful fanciful far-fetched implausible unbelievable unlikely

impromptu

(adjective) An impromptu action is one done without planning or organization.

e.g. *impromptu choruses of 'Happy Birthday'.*

ad-lib extempore improvised off the cuff spontaneous unpremeditated unprepared

improve

(verb) If something improves or if you improve it, it gets better or becomes more valuable.

e.g. *The weather had improved on the second day.*

ameliorate better correct develop enhance pick up polish progress upgrade

inactive

(adjective) not doing anything.

e.g. *An operation on his spine has kept him inactive.*

dormant idle immobile inert latent quiescent unemployed unoccupied unused

inadequate

(adjective) If something is inadequate, there is not enough of it, or it is not good enough in quality for a particular purpose.

e.g. *inadequate washing facilities.*

deficient imperfect incapable incomplete insufficient meagre poor scant sketchy skimpy sparse

inappropriate

(adjective) not suitable for a particular purpose or occasion.

e.g. *It was quite inappropriate to ask such questions.*

improper incongruous out of place tasteless unseemly unsuitable untimely wrong

incite

1. (verb) If you incite someone to do something, you encourage them to do it by making them angry or excited.

e.g. *The authorities incited a mob that burned down his house.*

drive egg on encourage goad inflame spur urge

2. If you incite trouble or violent behaviour, you encourage it by making people angry or excited.

e.g. *meetings which incite racial hatred.*

excite foment instigate provoke rouse stir up

include

(verb) If one thing includes another, it has the second thing as one of its parts.

e.g. *The price includes postage and package.*

comprehend comprise contain cover embrace encompass incorporate involve take in

incomparable

(adjective) Something that is incomparable is so good that it cannot be compared with anything else.

e.g. *castles of incomparable beauty.*

inimitable matchless paramount peerless superlative supreme unequalled unrivalled

inconsiderate

(adjective) If you are inconsiderate, you do not consider other people's feelings.

e.g. *a selfish, inconsiderate husband.*

careless insensitive tactless thoughtless unthinking

incredible

(adjective) totally amazing or impossible to believe.

e.g. *The fire spread at an incredible speed.*

amazing implausible impossible inconceivable preposterous unbelievable unimaginable unthinkable

independent

(adjective) Something that is independent happens or exists separately from other people or things.

e.g. *Results are assessed by an independent panel.*

autonomous self-sufficient separate unrelated

indicate

(verb) If something indicates something, it shows that it is true.

e.g. *a gesture which clearly indicates his relief.*

denote evince imply manifest reveal show signify suggest

indirect

1. (adjective) An indirect route, flight, etc. does not go in a straight line between two places and so takes a longer time.

e.g. *The goods went by a rather indirect route.*

circuitous devious meandering roundabout tortuous

2. An indirect answer, reference, etc. is one that does not directly mention the thing that is actually meant.

e.g. *Her indirect queries were met with more denial.*

circuitous oblique rambling roundabout

inexperienced

(adjective) lacking experience of a situation or activity.

e.g. *inexperienced drivers.*

amateur callow fresh green *informal* immature new raw unskilled

infectious

(adjective) spreading from one person to another.

e.g. *an infectious disease.*

catching contagious contaminating

inferior

1. (adjective) having a lower position or worth less than something else.

e.g. *inferior quality cassette tapes.*

bad lesser lower poor shoddy

2. (noun) Your inferiors are people in a lower position than you.

e.g. *We have never treated women as inferiors.*

junior subordinate

infinite

(adjective) without any limit or end.

e.g. *There could be an infinite number of universes.*

absolute boundless endless eternal limitless

influence

1. (noun) Influence is power that a person has over other people.

e.g. *These two guys had a great influence on my life.*

authority clout *informal* control effect hold leverage

power pull weight

2. (verb) To influence someone or something means to have an effect on them.

e.g. *It's all too easy to be influenced by your parents.*

affect bias direct guide persuade predispose sway

inform

1. (verb) If you inform someone of something, you tell them about it.

e.g. *He informed her of his decision.*

acquaint advise apprise enlighten notify tell

2. If you inform on a person, you tell the police about a crime they have committed.

e.g. *Christa discovered that her husband had been informing on her.*

sneak *informal* tell on

information

(noun) If you have information on or about something, you know something about it.

e.g. *Regional secretaries can provide information on local activities.*

data facts gen *informal* intelligence knowledge news report word

infrequent

(adjective) If something is infrequent it does not happen often.

e.g. *his infrequent letters.*

occasional rare sporadic uncommon unusual

ingratiate

(verb) If you ingratiate yourself with people, you try to make yourself popular with them, for example by always agreeing with them.

e.g. *He learned the skill of ingratiating himself with the right people.*

crawl curry favour fawn flatter grovel insinuate yourself toady

inhabitant

(noun) The inhabitants of a place are the people who live there.

e.g. *the inhabitants of Glasgow.*

citizen denizen local native resident

insincere

(adjective) Someone who is insincere pretends to have feelings which they do not really have.

e.g. *He says I'm the most insincere person he's ever met.*

artificial devious dishonest dissembling false hypocritical lying phoney shallow two-faced

insipid

(adjective) An insipid person or activity is dull and boring.

e.g. *this insipid Australian comedy.*

banal bland colourless drab dry dull flat lifeless prosaic spiritless tame tedious vapid wishy-washy

insult

1. (verb) If you insult someone, you offend them by being rude to them.

e.g. *The final straw came when Andrew insulted a woman teacher.*

abuse offend outrage slight snub

2. (noun) An insult is a rude remark which offends you.

e.g. *a racist insult.*

abuse affront indignity insolence offence outrage rudeness slight

integrate

1. (verb) If a person integrates into a group, they become part of it.

e.g. *schemes which assisted the refugees to integrate into the local economies.*

assimilate blend incorporate

2. To integrate things means to combine them so that they become closely linked or form part of a whole idea or system.

e.g. *his plan to integrate the coal and steel industries.*
coalesce combine fuse merge unite

intelligence

(noun) A person's intelligence is their ability to understand and learn things quickly and well.
e.g. *She had intelligence, ambition and drive.*
brains cleverness intellect mind reason understanding

interfere

(verb) If you interfere in a situation, you try to influence it, although it does not really concern you.
e.g. *He urged the French government not to interfere in German affairs.*
butt in intervene intrude meddle poke your nose in tamper

interrogate

(verb) If you interrogate someone, you question them thoroughly to get information from them.
e.g. *The police arrested and interrogated him.*
cross-examine examine grill pump question quiz

interval

(noun) An interval is a short break during a play or concert.
e.g. *The cost of the ticket includes a glass of champagne during the interval.*
break interlude intermission

intervene

(verb) If you intervene in a situation, you step in to prevent conflict between people.
e.g. *Police had intervened to try to stop protesters.*
arbitrate intercede mediate

intonation

(noun) Your intonation is the way that your voice rises and falls as you speak.

e.g. *his father's Austrian intonation.*

cadence inflection modulation

introduction

(noun) The introduction to a book is a piece of writing at the beginning of it, which usually discusses the book in some detail.

e.g. *a memorable passage in the introduction to his 'Collected Poems'.*

foreword opening preamble preface prologue

intrude

(verb) To intrude on someone or something means to disturb them.

e.g. *I don't want to intrude on your parents.*

barge in *informal* encroach gatecrash interrupt trespass

invent

1. (verb) If you invent a machine, device, or process, you are the first person to think of it or to use it.

e.g. *The hot-dog was invented in Coney Island by Charles Feltman.*

coin conceive create design devise discover formulate originate

2. If you invent a story or an excuse, you make it up.

e.g. *He had invented an imaginary son.*

imagine improvise make up

investigate

(verb) To investigate something means to try to find out all the facts about it.

e.g. *Gas board engineers were investigating the incident.*

examine explore follow up look into make inquiries probe search sift

invincible

(adjective) unable to be defeated.

e.g. *an invincible army.*

indestructible indomitable insuperable unbeatable

irregular

(adjective) Something that is irregular is not smooth or straight, or does not form a regular pattern.

e.g. *The paint was drying in irregular patches.*

asymmetrical broken eccentric erratic fitful fluctuating fragmentary haphazard intermittent occasional patchy random shifting spasmodic sporadic variable wavering

irresponsible

(adjective) An irresponsible person does things without considering the consequences.

e.g. *an irresponsible driver.*

careless feckless reckless thoughtless wild

irritate

(verb) If something irritates you, it annoys you.

e.g. *He irritated her by eating all the cream.*

aggravate anger annoy bother chafe exasperate fret gall grate infuriate jar nettle pester provoke ruffle vex

issue

1. (noun) An issue is an important subject that people are talking about.

e.g. *the issues at stake.*

affair argument concern matter point problem question subject topic

2. (verb) If someone issues something, they officially supply it.

e.g. *I was issued with a prison uniform.*

distribute give out supply

item

1. (noun) An item is one of a collection or list of things.

e.g. *The first item he bought was an alarm clock.*

aspect component consideration detail entry matter particular point thing

2. An item is a newspaper or magazine article.

e.g. *an item on how to take carnation cuttings.*

account article feature piece report

J j

jagged

(adjective) sharp and spiky.

e.g. *He tore his coat on a jagged piece of metal.*

ragged serrated sharp spiked

jail

(noun) A jail is a building where people convicted of a crime are locked up.

e.g. *He spent six months in jail for burglary.*

clink *slang* jug *slang* nick *British slang* penitentiary *U.S.* prison

jam

(noun) If someone is in a jam, they are in a difficult situation.

e.g. *I'm in the same financial jam as you are.*

fix *informal* pickle *informal* plight predicament quandary trouble

jealous

1. (adjective) If you are jealous of someone, you feel bitterness and anger towards them because of something they possess or something they have achieved.

e.g. *They're just jealous of your success.*

covetous envious grudging resentful

2. If you are jealous of something you have, you feel you must try to keep it from other people.

e.g. *He was a very jealous husband.*

possessive

jewel

(noun) A jewel is a precious stone used to decorate valuable ornaments or jewellery.

e.g. *a rare and irreplaceable jewel.*

gem gemstone

jinks

(noun) High jinks is boisterous and mischievous behaviour.

e.g. *Bill's annual parties are notorious for high jinks.*

fun and games merrymaking

job

(noun) A job is the work that someone does to earn money.

e.g. *He thought he might lose his job.*

employment livelihood occupation office position post profession situation trade work

join

1. (verb) When two things join, or when one thing joins another, they come together.

e.g. *This road joins the motorway at junction 16.*

adhere connect couple link unite

2. If you join a club or organization, you become a member of it or start taking part in it.

e.g. *He joined the company ten years ago.*

enlist enrol enter sign up

3. To join two things means to fasten them.

e.g. *Join the two outside edges together.*

add cement connect couple fasten link unite

joke

1. (noun) A joke is something that you say or do to make people laugh, such as a funny story.

e.g. *Kennedy chipped in with a good joke.*

gag *informal* hoax jest prank quip wisecrack *informal* witticism

2. (verb) If you are joking, you are teasing someone.
e.g. *Don't take her seriously, she was only joking.*
chaff jest kid *informal* tease wind up *British slang*

journey

(noun) A journey is the act of travelling from one place to another.
e.g. *a long day's journey there and back.*
excursion expedition trip voyage

judge

1. (noun) A judge is someone who decides the winner in a contest or competition.
e.g. *The judges awarded him first place.*
adjudicator arbiter referee umpire

2. (verb) To judge a contest or competition means to decide on the winner.
e.g. *She judges at dog shows all over the country.*
adjudge adjudicate referee umpire

jump

1. (verb) To jump means to spring off the ground or some other surface using your leg muscles.
e.g. *She tried to jump out of the window.*
bound leap spring

2. To jump something means to spring off the ground and move over or across it.
e.g. *He jumped the fence and ran for his life.*
clear hurdle vault

3. (noun) A jump is a spring into the air, sometimes over an object.
e.g. *a jump of 2.37 metres.*
bound leap spring

jut

(verb) If something juts out, it sticks out beyond or above a surface or edge.

e.g. *jagged rocks jutting out of the sea.*

project   protrude   stick out

K k

keen

(adjective) Someone who is keen shows great eagerness and enthusiasm.

e.g. *a keen gardener.*

ardent avid eager earnest enthusiastic zealous

keep

1. (verb) To keep someone or something in a particular condition means to make them stay in that condition.

e.g. *We'll walk to keep warm.*

conserve hold maintain preserve retain store uphold

2. If you keep something, you have it and look after it.

e.g. *a gun that he kept for his private use.*

carry look after possess safeguard

keepsake

(noun) A keepsake is something that someone gives you to remind you of a particular person or event.

e.g. *a rare picture of his father for a keepsake.*

memento relic reminder souvenir symbol token

kidnap

(verb) To kidnap someone means to take them away by force and demand a ransom in exchange for returning them.

e.g. *He'd been kidnapped for money.*

abduct capture hijack seize snatch

kill

(verb) To kill a person, animal, or plant means to make them die.

e.g. *I couldn't kill a cat.*
annihilate assassinate butcher destroy dispatch execute exterminate extirpate massacre murder obliterate slaughter slay

kin

(plural noun) Your kin are your relatives.
e.g. *The reasons for moving were to be nearer kin or friends.*
family kinsfolk relations relatives

kind

1. (noun) A particular kind of thing is something of the same type or sort as other things.
e.g. *I don't like that kind of film.*
brand class sort species stamp type variety

2. (adjective) Someone who is kind is considerate and generous towards other people.
e.g. *There was a kind and understanding side to him.*
benevolent benign kindhearted magnanimous

king

(noun) The king of a country is a man who is the head of state in the country, and who inherited his position from his parents.
e.g. *George became King in 1936.*
monarch ruler sovereign

knowledge

(noun) Knowledge is all the information and facts that you know.
e.g. *professors of great knowledge.*
enlightenment instruction intelligence know-how learning scholarship science tuition wisdom

L l

labour

1. (noun) Labour is hard work.
e.g. *Technology has taken a lot of the hard labour out of housework.*
drudgery effort exertion industry slog *informal* toil travail

2. (verb; an old-fashioned use) To labour means to work hard.
e.g. *We laboured for three quarters of an hour.*
slave slog *informal* toil travail work

lack

(noun) If there is a lack of something, it is not present when or where it is needed.
e.g. *They complained of the lack of safety provisions.*
absence dearth deficiency paucity scarcity shortage want

lag

(verb) To lag behind means to make slower progress than other people or processes.
e.g. *Britain still lags far behind other countries in engineering.*
dawdle fall behind linger loiter straggle trail

lame

(adjective) A lame excuse is weak and unconvincing.
e.g. *He mumbled some lame excuse about having gone to sleep.*
feeble flimsy inadequate pathetic poor thin weak

lament

(verb) To lament something means to express sorrow or regret about it.
e.g. *He laments the demise of cricket playing in schools.*

bemoan bewail complain deplore grieve mourn regret sorrow wail weep

language

(noun) Your language is the style in which you express yourself.

e.g. *His language is often obscure.*

idiom lingo parlance speech style vocabulary wording

lanky

(adjective) Someone who is lanky is tall and thin and moves rather awkwardly.

e.g. *He leaned his lanky body over the desk.*

angular bony gangling gaunt spare tall thin

last

1. (verb) If something lasts, it continues to exist or happen.

e.g. *Her speech lasted for fifty minutes.*

continue endure go on hold out remain survive

2. (adjective) Something or someone who is last is the latest or most recent in a series.

e.g. *The last customers left at midnight.*

closing concluding final hindmost latest

late

(adjective) If something or someone is late, they are after the expected or usual time.

e.g. *a late lunch at the hotel.*

behind belated delayed overdue slow tardy

latent

(adjective) A latent quality is hidden at the moment, but may emerge in the future.

e.g. *a latent talent for drawing.*

dormant potential unrealized

layabout

(noun; an informal word) A layabout is someone who is lazy and does not work.

e.g. *He is a morose, work-shy layabout.*

good-for-nothing idler laggard loafer vagrant

layer

(noun) A layer is a single thickness of something.

e.g. *layers of clothing.*

coat ply row seam sheet stratum thickness tier

layout

(noun) The layout of something is the pattern in which it is arranged.

e.g. *He tried to recall the layout of the farmhouse.*

arrangement design draft format outline plan

laze

(verb) If you laze, you relax and do no work.

e.g. *We spent a few days lazing around by the pool.*

idle loaf loll lounge relax take it easy *informal*

lazy

(adjective) idle and unwilling to work.

e.g. *He is too lazy to get up in the morning.*

idle indolent lethargic shiftless slack slothful

lead

1. (verb) If you lead someone somewhere, you go in front of them in order to show them the way.

e.g. *He led her to a vacant table.*

conduct escort guide pilot precede steer usher

2. Someone who leads a group of people is in charge of them.

e.g. *The Labour Party was led by Wilson.*

command direct govern head manage preside over supervise

learn

(verb) If you learn of something, you find out about it.

e.g. *She learnt of his death from his sister.*

detect discern discover find find out gather grasp hear pick up understand

learned

1. (adjective) A learned person has a lot of knowledge gained from years of study.

e.g. *a learned professor.*

cultured erudite expert scholarly

2. Learned books and journals are written about serious academic subjects.

e.g. *a stream of articles in learned journals.*

academic highbrow

least

(noun) The least is the smallest possible amount of something.

e.g. *No one paid the least attention to him.*

fewest lowest minimal minimum slightest tiniest

leave

(verb) When you leave a place, you go away from it.

e.g. *He decided to leave Paris.*

decamp depart desert disappear exit go move quit relinquish retire withdraw

legacy

(noun) A legacy is property or money that someone receives in the will of a person who has died.

e.g. *a legacy left to me by my uncle.*

bequest estate heirloom inheritance

leisurely

(adjective) A leisurely action is done in an unhurried and calm way.

e.g. *a leisurely stroll.*

comfortable easy gentle lazy relaxed restful slow unhurried

lengthen

(verb) To lengthen something means to make it longer.

e.g. *I lengthened my stride.*

elongate expand extend prolong protract stretch

lessen

(verb) If something lessens, it is reduced in amount, size, or quality.

e.g. *The wind's noise lessened.*

abate decline decrease deplete diminish dwindle lighten reduce relax shrink slacken wane weaken

let

(verb) If you let someone do something, you allow them to do it.

e.g. *Don't let other people take advantage of you.*

allow authorize give permission permit sanction

lethargic

(adjective) If you feel lethargic, you have no energy or enthusiasm.

e.g. *She became pale and lethargic.*

apathetic drowsy dull heavy inactive languid listless slothful slow sluggish somnolent torpid

level

1. (adjective) A surface that is level is smooth and flat.

e.g. *She looked across absolutely level fields.*

even flat horizontal smooth

2. (noun) A level is a point on a scale which measures the amount, importance, or difficulty of something.

e.g. *the highest level of government.*

degree grade rank stage step

lie

1. (verb) To lie means to say something that is not true.
e.g. *She lied about her age.*
equivocate fabricate fib prevaricate

2. (noun) A lie is something you say which is not true.
e.g. *She told lies as often as she told the truth.*
fabrication falsehood fib prevarication untruth

lift

1. (verb) To lift something means to move it to a higher position.
e.g. *She lifted the mug and took a long swallow.*
elevate hoist mount pick up raise

2. To lift a ban on something means to remove it.
e.g. *to lift all controls on textile imports.*
annul cancel end relax remove rescind revoke stop

light

1. (noun) Light is brightness from the sun, moon, fire, or lamps, that enables you to see things.
e.g. *the light of the moon.*
brilliance glow illumination lighting radiance

2. (verb) To light a fire means to make it start burning.
e.g. *They were lighting oil-lamps, torches and candles.*
fire ignite kindle set fire to

3. (adjective) A light object does not weigh very much.
e.g. *She was as light as a feather.*
airy delicate flimsy insubstantial lightweight portable slight underweight

4. A light task is fairly easy.
e.g. *I've been doing a little light training.*
easy effortless manageable moderate simple undemanding

light-hearted

(adjective) Someone who is light-hearted is cheerful and has no worries.

e.g. *George can be a light-hearted character.*

blithe carefree cheerful chirpy happy-go-lucky sunny untroubled

like

1. (verb) If you like something or someone, you find them pleasant.

e.g. *He likes classical music.*

be fond of be keen on be partial to care for enjoy

2. (preposition) If one thing is like another, it is similar to it.

e.g. *I saw a dog like ours on the beach.*

akin alike allied analogous corresponding identical relating resembling same similar

limit

(noun) A limit is a boundary or an extreme beyond which something cannot go.

e.g. *The speed limit was 30 mph.*

bound boundary ceiling check curb deadline end extent maximum restraint restriction

liquid

(adjective) Something that is liquid is in the form of a liquid.

e.g. *liquid nitrogen.*

fluid melted molten running runny thawed watery

list

1. (noun) A list is a set of words or items written one below the other.

e.g. *a shopping list.*

catalogue directory file inventory register roll schedule tally

2. (verb) If you list a number of things, you make a list of

them.

e.g. *Manufacturers will have to list all ingredients on the label.*

catalogue enter enumerate file index itemize note record register

literal

(adjective) A literal translation from a foreign language is one that has been translated exactly word for word.

e.g. *The literal meaning of contre-jour is 'against day'.*

exact faithful strict verbatim word for word

little

(adjective) small in size or amount.

e.g. *little bottles of shampoo and shower gel.*

diminutive mini miniature minute petite pygmy small tiny wee

live

(verb) If you live in a place, that is where your home is.

e.g. *My sister lives in Ulster.*

abide dwell inhabit lodge reside settle stay

lively

(adjective) full of life and enthusiasm.

e.g. *a lively debate.*

active brisk bustling busy colourful crowded eventful exciting frisky perky racy spirited stimulating stirring vivacious vivid

loan

1. (noun) A loan is a sum of money that you borrow.

e.g. *a loan from the bank.*

advance credit

2. (verb) If you loan something to someone, you lend it to them.

e.g. *I loaned them some clothes.*

advance lend

local

1. (adjective) Local means in, near, or belonging to the area in which you live.

e.g. *the local newspaper.*

community district neighbourhood regional

2. (noun) The locals are the people who live in a particular area.

e.g. *The locals view the proposal with alarm.*

inhabitant native resident

location

(noun) A location is a place, or the position of something.

e.g. *the perfect location for a hotel.*

place point position site situation venue whereabouts

lone

(adjective) A lone person or thing is the only one in a particular place.

e.g. *a lone climber.*

isolated single sole solitary solo unaccompanied

long

1. (adjective) continuing for a great amount of time.

e.g. *There had been no rain for a long time.*

drawn-out extended lengthy prolonged protracted

2. (verb) If you long for something, you want it very much.

e.g. *She longs to join an amateur dramatics class.*

pine wish yearn

long-winded

(adjective) long and boring.

e.g. *a long-winded letter.*

garrulous lengthy rambling repetitious tedious verbose wordy

look

1. (verb) If you look at something, you turn your eyes towards it so that you can see it.

e.g. *Taggart looked at his watch.*

behold contemplate gaze glance inspect observe peek peep regard scrutinize view

2. (noun) If you have a look at something, you look at it.

e.g. *I had a quick look round the place.*

glance glimpse peek peep sight

3. The look on your face is the expression on it.

e.g. *a look of surprise.*

appearance aspect countenance demeanour expression

loosen

(verb) To loosen something means to make it looser.

e.g. *He loosened his collar.*

free slacken undo unfasten untie

loot

1. (verb) To loot shops and houses means to steal money and goods from them during a battle or riot.

e.g. *Angry workers looted shops.*

pillage plunder raid ransack sack

2. (noun) Loot is stolen money or goods.

e.g. *bags that looked to be full of loot.*

booty haul prize spoils swag

lost

(adjective) If something is lost, you cannot find it.

e.g. *golfers looking for lost balls.*

astray disappeared gone mislaid misplaced missing vanished

lot

(noun) A lot of something, or lots of something, is a large

amount of it.

e.g. *a vegetarian diet including a lot of pasta.*

abundance heaps loads many masses oodles piles plenty quantities scores

loud

1. (adjective) A loud noise has a high volume of sound.

e.g. *a loud explosion.*

blaring deafening noisy piercing raucous resounding rowdy sonorous stentorian *formal* strong

2. If you describe clothing as loud, you mean that it is too bright and tasteless.

e.g. *a loud checked shirt.*

flamboyant flashy garish gaudy lurid ostentatious showy tacky tasteless vulgar

love

1. (verb) If you love someone, you have strong emotional feelings of affection for them.

e.g. *He loved his wife and his children.*

adore cherish dote on idolize prize treasure worship

2. (noun) Love is a strong feeling of affection for someone or something.

e.g. *a genuine love of literature.*

adulation affection ardour devotion fondness friendship infatuation liking passion rapture regard tenderness warmth

lovely

(adjective) Very beautiful, attractive, and pleasant.

e.g. *the lovely old manor house.*

attractive beautiful charming delightful enchanting exquisite pleasant pretty

lower

(adjective) Lower describes people and things that are less

important than other people and things.

e.g. *clubs in the lower divisions.*

junior lesser minor secondary smaller subordinate

luck

(noun) Luck is anything that seems to happen by chance and not through your own efforts.

e.g. *I found my way there by luck.*

accident chance destiny fate fluke fortune prosperity success windfall

lucky

1. (adjective) Someone who is lucky has a lot of good luck.

e.g. *He had always been lucky at cards.*

charmed favoured fortunate

2. Something that is lucky happens by chance and has good effects or consequences.

e.g. *a lucky escape.*

auspicious fortuitous fortunate opportune propitious

lustful

(adjective) feeling or expressing strong sexual desire.

e.g. *lustful thoughts.*

lascivious lecherous lewd licentious prurient salacious

luxurious

(adjective) very expensive and full of luxury.

e.g. *The rooms were furnished with luxurious carpets.*

costly expensive lavish opulent rich splendid sumptuous

luxury

(noun) A luxury is something that you enjoy very much but do not have very often, usually because it is expensive.

e.g. *the luxury of breakfast in bed.*

extra extravagance indulgence treat

lying

(adjective) A lying person often tells lies.
e.g. *He is a lying scoundrel!*
deceitful dishonest false mendacious untruthful

M m

machine

(noun) A machine is a piece of equipment which uses electricity or power from an engine.

e.g. *a technician in white who sat next to a large noisy machine.*

apparatus appliance contrivance device structure

mad

1. (adjective) Someone who is mad has a mental illness which often causes them to behave in strange ways.

e.g. *They'd say she was mad, or, worse, she was making it up.*

demented deranged insane unbalanced unhinged

2. If you describe someone as mad, you mean that they are very foolish.

e.g. *You must be mad to go out there alone.*

crazy foolhardy foolish imprudent senseless

magic

(noun) Magic is the art of performing tricks to entertain people.

e.g. *We're trying to find someone to do some magic at the children's party.*

conjuring illusion sleight of hand sorcery trickery witchcraft

main

(adjective) most important.

e.g. *a main road.*

central chief critical crucial essential foremost head leading major premier primary prime principal

majority

(noun) The majority of people or things in a group is more than half of the group.

e.g. *The majority of the electorate were illiterate.*

best part bulk mass preponderance

make

1. (verb) To make something means to produce or construct it, or to cause it to happen.

e.g. *In your place I should not make any sweeping changes.*

accomplish assemble build compose construct create fabricate fashion form generate manufacture originate produce

2. If someone makes you do something, they force you to do it.

e.g. *She makes us wash up.*

coerce compel constrain dragoon drive force impel induce oblige

3. (noun) The make of a product is the name of the company that manufactured it.

e.g. *'What make is your car?' -- 'It's a Datsun.'*

brand kind model type

makeshift

(adjective) temporary and of poor quality.

e.g. *The refugees were put into makeshift shelters.*

provisional stopgap temporary

making

(noun) The making of something is the act or process of creating or producing it.

e.g. *The making of the wine needs skill and full attention.*

assembly building construction creation manufacture production

malevolent

(adjective; a formal word) wanting or intending to cause harm.

e.g. *Her stare was malevolent, her mouth a thin line.*
baleful hostile malicious malign malignant pernicious spiteful vengeful vicious vindictive

malice

(noun) Malice is a desire to cause harm to people.
e.g. *He could be ruthless, but there was no malice in him.*
animosity bitterness enmity hate hatred ill will malevolence rancour spite venom vindictiveness

man

1. (noun) A man is an adult male human being.
e.g. *The young man stopped at the side of the road.*
bloke *informal* chap *informal* fellow gentleman guy *informal* male

2. (plural noun) Human beings in general are sometimes referred to as men.
e.g. *All men are equal.*
humanity mankind mortals people

manage

(verb) If you manage to do something, you succeed in doing it.
e.g. *However did you manage to find me?*
accomplish arrange contrive cope effect engineer get by succeed survive

management

(noun) The management of a business is the controlling and organizing of it.
e.g. *involvement in the management of local government.*
administration control running supervision

manner

1. (noun) The manner in which you do something is the way in which you do it.
e.g. *to behave in a more socially responsible manner.*

fashion method mode style system technique way

2. Your manner is the way in which you behave and talk.

e.g. *The judge was impressed by his manner.*

air appearance approach attitude bearing behaviour conduct demeanour deportment look presence tone

marine

(adjective) relating to or involving the sea.

e.g. *marine life.*

maritime nautical naval oceanic seafaring

marital

(adjective) relating to or involving marriage.

e.g. *marital problems.*

conjugal married matrimonial wedded

market

(noun) A market is a place where goods or animals are bought and sold.

e.g. *Bargaining, except in the odd market or antique shop, is no longer appropriate.*

bazaar fair mart

marriage

(noun) Marriage is the act of marrying someone.

e.g. *a mixture of regret and happiness at her daughter's marriage.*

alliance matrimony union wedding wedlock

matter

1. (noun) A matter is something that you have to deal with.

e.g. *I have given the matter much thought.*

affair business concern episode incident issue question situation subject topic

2. (verb) If something matters to you, it is important.

e.g. *The wallpaper really did not matter a lot to him.*

be important count signify

mean

1. (verb) If you mean to do something, you intend to do it.

e.g. *Sorry, I meant to write before.*

intend plan propose want wish

2. (adjective) Someone who is mean is unwilling to spend much money.

e.g. *Don't be mean with the tip.*

miserly niggardly parsimonious stingy tight tight-fisted

meaning

(noun) The meaning of what someone says, or of a book or a film, is the thoughts or ideas that it is intended to express.

e.g. *Mark was old enough now to understand their meaning.*

content drift explanation gist implication import interpretation message point sense significance substance

mediocre

(adjective) of rather poor quality.

e.g. *a mediocre string of performances.*

average indifferent middling ordinary passable pedestrian so-so tolerable undistinguished uninspired

meek

(adjective) A meek person is timid and does what other people say.

e.g. *holding out his sword in meek surrender.*

acquiescent compliant deferential docile gentle humble mild modest submissive yielding

meet

(verb) If you meet someone, you happen to be in the same place as them.

e.g. *We met her at the hotel.*

bump into come across confront contact encounter find

meeting

(noun) A meeting is an event in which people discuss proposals and make decisions together.

e.g. *the association's annual meeting.*

assembly conference convention gathering get-together session

melodious

(adjective) pleasant to listen to.

e.g. *soft melodious music.*

dulcet mellifluous musical silvery sweet-sounding tuneful

melodramatic

(adjective) behaving in an exaggerated, emotional way.

e.g. *She wanted to laugh at the melodramatic way he was behaving.*

dramatic extravagant histrionic theatrical

melt

(verb) When something melts or when you melt it, it changes from a solid to a liquid because it has been heated.

e.g. *watching the mounds of snow melt in the courtyard.*

dissolve liquefy soften thaw

memory

(noun) A memory is something you remember about the past.

e.g. *childhood memories.*

recollection remembrance reminiscence

mention

(verb) If you mention something, you talk about it briefly.

e.g. *She told me something then that Tim had never mentioned.*

allude bring up broach cite refer to

merchandise

(noun; a formal word) Merchandise is goods that are sold.

e.g. *He had left me with more merchandise than I could sell.*

commodities goods produce products stock wares

merchant

(noun) A merchant is a trader who imports and exports goods.

e.g. *a textile merchant.*

dealer retailer purveyor salesman supplier trader vendor

merciful

(adjective) showing kindness and forgiveness.

e.g. *It's the most merciful way there is.*

compassionate forbearing forgiving gracious humane kind lenient sparing

merciless

(adjective) showing no kindness or forgiveness.

e.g. *calling for the merciless elimination of enemy commando units.*

heartless implacable inexorable pitiless relentless remorseless ruthless unfeeling

mercy

(noun) If you show mercy, you show kindness and forgiveness and do not punish someone as severely as you could.

e.g. *There was no thought of mercy, only of revenge.*

clemency compassion forbearance forgiveness leniency pity quarter

merriment

(noun) Merriment is happiness, laughter, and fun.

e.g. *As midnight drew near, merriment waxed fierce and furious.*

amusement conviviality festivity fun gaiety glee hilarity jollity laughter mirth revelry

mess

1. (noun) If something is a mess, it is untidy.
e.g. *They make a terrible mess when they're here.*
chaos clutter confusion disarray disorder hash *informal* jumble shambles untidiness

2. If a situation is a mess, it is full of problems and trouble.
e.g. *Edwards was already sorry he had got himself into this mess.*
difficulty dilemma fix *informal* jam *informal* mix-up muddle pickle *informal* predicament

messenger

(noun) A messenger is someone who takes a message to someone for someone else.
e.g. *A messenger delivered an envelope at the office.*
courier emissary envoy go-between

mild

(adjective) Mild weather is warmer than usual.
e.g. *We've had two mild winters.*
balmy clement temperate warm

miserable

1. (adjective) If you are miserable, you are very unhappy.
e.g. *Now everything's gone wrong and I feel helpless and miserable.*
dejected depressed despondent disconsolate distressed doleful downcast gloomy lugubrious melancholy mournful sorrowful unhappy woebegone wretched

2. If a place or a situation is miserable, it makes you feel depressed.
e.g. *a squalid, miserable little bed-sit.*
depressing dismal gloomy poor shabby sordid squalid wretched

mistake

(noun) A mistake is an action or opinion that is wrong or is not what you intended.

e.g. *Annoyed, he realized he had made a mistake.*
blunder error fault faux pas gaffe misunderstanding oversight slip solecism

mix

(verb) If you mix things, you combine them or shake or stir them together.
e.g. *I don't like mixing business and pleasure.*
amalgamate blend combine merge mingle

mixture

(noun) A mixture of things consists of several different things put together.
e.g. *Alan looked at him with a mixture of incredulity and fear.*
alloy amalgam assortment blend combination compound concoction conglomeration medley miscellany mix variety

mock

1. (verb) If you mock someone, you say something scornful or imitate their foolish behaviour.
e.g. *Sometimes they mocked her, calling out behind her back.*
deride gibe jeer make fun of ridicule scoff sneer taunt wind up *informal*

2. (adjective) not genuine.
e.g. *mock Tudor houses.*
artificial fake imitation sham spurious

mockery

(noun) Mockery is the expression of scorn for someone or ridicule of their foolish behaviour.
e.g. *He looked impressed, but was there a glint of mockery in his eyes?*
contempt derision jeering ridicule scorn

model

(noun) Something that is described as, for example, a model of clarity or a model of perfection, is extremely clear or absolutely perfect.

e.g. *This garment, which was already a model of neatness, was straightened out.*

archetype epitome example ideal paragon pattern prototype standard

modern

1. (adjective) relating to the present time.

e.g. *the social problems of modern society.*

contemporary current present-day

2. new and involving the latest ideas and equipment.

e.g. *modern technology.*

latest new present up-to-date

moment

(noun) A moment is a very short period of time.

e.g. *She hesitated for a moment.*

instant jiffy minute second

money

(noun) Money is the coins or banknotes that you use to buy something.

e.g. *Jim bought a house with the money.*

capital cash currency funds

mood

1. (noun) Your mood is the way you are feeling at a particular time.

e.g. *I'm in a really good mood.*

frame of mind humour temper

2. The mood of a group of people is the way they think or feel about something.

e.g. *A mood of pessimism grew amongst the delegates.*

air atmosphere tenor vein

moody

1. (adjective) Someone who is moody is depressed or unhappy.

e.g. *retreating into moody silence.*

gloomy glum morose petulant sulky sullen

2. Someone who is moody often changes their mood for no apparent reason.

e.g. *This type of personality can be moody and difficult.*

temperamental touchy

motivate

(verb) If you are motivated by something, it causes you to behave in a particular way.

e.g. *people motivated by a lust for power and money.*

actuate drive impel induce inspire move prompt stimulate

move

1. (verb) To move means to go to a different place or position..

e.g. *Can you move down the bus, please?*

budge go proceed stir walk

2. To move something means to change its place or position.

e.g. *Workmen were moving a heavy wardrobe.*

carry shift transport

muddle

1. (noun) A muddle is a state of disorder or untidiness.

e.g. *My papers are all in a muddle.*

chaos clutter confusion disarray disorder hotchpotch mess mix-up tangle

2. (verb) If you muddle things, you mix them up.

e.g. *The work became hopelessly muddled.*

confuse jumble mix up

murder

(noun) Murder is the deliberate and unlawful killing of a person.
e.g. *investigating the murder of the MP.*
assassination bloodshed homicide killing slaughter

murmur

1. (verb) If you murmur, you say something very softly.
e.g. *Across the room she sensed that her mother murmured something to John.*
mumble mutter whisper

2. (noun) A murmur is an utterance which can hardly be heard.
e.g. *The sergeants spoke in low murmurs.*
babble buzz drone humming muttering purr rumble undertone whisper

musical

(adjective) Musical sounds are pleasant and tuneful.
e.g. *His voice was soft and soothing, almost musical.*
dulcet harmonious lilting lyrical melodious tuneful

mysterious

1. (adjective) strange and not well understood.
e.g. *a mysterious phenomenon known as corn circles.*
abstruse arcane baffling curious inexplicable obscure recondite secret strange uncanny weird

2. secretive about something.
e.g. *You've been very mysterious lately; what's going on?*
cryptic enigmatic furtive

N n

narrow-minded

(adjective) unwilling to consider new ideas or opinions.

e.g. *I'm not too narrow-minded in my outlook.*

bigoted hidebound insular narrow parochial

nasty

(adjective) very unpleasant.

e.g. *Ella spat out the name as if it had a nasty taste.*

disagreeable disgusting foul horrible loathsome nauseating objectionable odious offensive repellent repugnant unpleasant vile

natural

1. (adjective) not trying to pretend or hide anything.

e.g. *talking in a relaxed, natural manner.*

artless candid frank genuine ingenuous open real simple spontaneous unaffected

2. A natural ability is one you were born with.

e.g. *her natural talent for singing.*

inborn inherent innate instinctive intuitive native

naval

(adjective) relating to or having a navy.

e.g. *naval bases.*

marine maritime nautical

necessary

(adjective) Something that is necessary is needed or must be done.

e.g. *harsh but necessary measures.*

compulsory essential imperative mandatory needful obligatory required requisite vital

need

(noun) Your needs are the things that you need to have.

e.g. *Shoes are needs, not luxuries.*

demand essential necessity requirement requisite want

needless

(adjective) unnecessary.

e.g. *needless cruelty.*

gratuitous groundless pointless redundant superfluous uncalled-for

nervous

(adjective) worried and frightened.

e.g. *I felt very nervous about travelling.*

agitated anxious apprehensive edgy fearful fidgety jittery *informal* jumpy neurotic on edge tense uptight worried

new

1. (adjective) recently made or created.

e.g. *a new plan.*

brand-new different fresh improved latest modern modernized newfangled novel up-to-date

2. not known, used, or encountered before.

e.g. *a part of England completely new to her.*

unfamiliar unknown virgin

next

(adjective) coming immediately after something else.

e.g. *They lived in the next street.*

adjacent adjoining consequent ensuing following later neighbouring subsequent succeeding

nice

(adjective) pleasant or attractive.

e.g. *He's such a nice young man.*

agreeable attractive charming delightful good likable pleasant

nobility

(noun) The nobility of a society are all the people who have titles and high social rank.

e.g. *The nobility retained its social influence.*

aristocracy nobles peerage peers upper classes

noise

(noun) A noise is a sound, especially one that is loud or unpleasant.

e.g. *The children make a dreadful noise.*

clamour commotion din hubbub pandemonium racket row sound tumult uproar

nominate

(verb) If you nominate someone for a job or position, you formally suggest that they have it.

e.g. *candidates who had been nominated for the programme.*

assign designate name propose recommend suggest

nonsense

(noun) Nonsense is foolish and meaningless words or behaviour.

e.g. *Don't talk nonsense.*

absurdity bilge *informal* bombast drivel folly rot rubbish stupidity trash twaddle

normal

(adjective) usual and ordinary.

e.g. *I try to lead a normal life.*

average natural ordinary routine typical usual

notice

1. (verb) If you notice something, you become aware of it.

e.g. *We all noticed an improvement.*

detect discern distinguish heed mind note observe perceive see spot

2. (noun) Notice is attention or awareness.

e.g. *I'm glad he brought it to my notice.*

attention observation

notorious

(adjective) well-known for something bad.

e.g. *The area has become notorious for violence against tourists.*

disreputable infamous scandalous

nuisance

(noun) A nuisance is someone or something that is annoying or inconvenient.

e.g. *Our dog was causing a nuisance by barking.*

bore bother drag *informal* hassle inconvenience irritation pest problem trouble vexation

number

(noun) A number is a word or a symbol used for counting or calculating.

e.g. *the numbers one, two, and three.*

digit figure numeral

O o

oaf

(noun) An oaf is a clumsy and stupid person.

e.g. *He was irascible and earthy, something of an oaf.*

boor brute lout

oath

(noun) An oath is a formal promise, especially a promise to tell the truth in a court of law.

e.g. *They were ready to swear on oath that Cantrell had known about it.*

avowal pledge vow

obese

(adjective) extremely fat.

e.g. *He has become obese and lazy.*

corpulent fat fleshy gross heavy outsize plump podgy portly rotund stout

obey

(verb) If you obey a person or an order, you do what you are told to do.

e.g. *All visitors must obey the rules.*

abide by comply conform discharge execute follow fulfil heed keep mind observe perform respond

object

(verb) If you object to something, you dislike it or disapprove of it.

e.g. *Politicians of all parties objected to the way the article questioned their patriotism and resolve.*

demur expostulate oppose protest take exception

obscene

(adjective) indecent and offensive.

e.g. *obscene pictures.*

bawdy blue coarse dirty disgusting filthy foul immoral improper impure indecent lewd offensive pornographic salacious suggestive

obscure

(adjective) Something obscure is difficult to see or to understand.

e.g. *The news was shrouded in obscure language.*

abstruse arcane confusing cryptic deep mysterious opaque recondite unclear

obsession

(noun) If someone has an obsession about something, they cannot stop thinking about that thing.

e.g. *Antiques were his obsession.*

fetish fixation mania phobia preoccupation thing *informal*

obsolete

(adjective) out of date and no longer used.

e.g. *The original concept of limited war had been rendered obsolete by changing political circumstances.*

antiquated archaic bygone dated defunct extinct outmoded passé

obstacle

(noun) An obstacle is something which is in your way and makes it difficult to do something.

e.g. *The price was also something of an obstacle.*

bar barrier block check hindrance hitch hurdle obstruction stumbling block

obstinate

(adjective) Someone who is obstinate is stubborn and unwilling to change their mind.

e.g. *She is a very strong-willed child and can be very obstinate.*
determined dogged immovable inflexible intractable intransigent pig-headed stubborn unyielding

obvious

(adjective) easy to see or understand.
e.g. *"All right," he said with obvious reluctance.*
apparent blatant clear conspicuous distinct evident manifest overt palpable patent perceptible plain pronounced transparent unmistakable

oddments

(plural noun) Oddments are things that are left over after other things have been used.
e.g. *She filled it with oddments that she fancied might be useful on the journey.*
odds and ends remnants

offer

(verb) If you offer something to someone, you ask them if they would like it.
e.g. *He looked as if he too would gladly offer help.*
proffer suggest tender volunteer

ogle

(verb) To ogle someone means to stare at them in a way that indicates a sexual interest.
e.g. *spitting tobacco juice and ogling the passing ladies.*
eye up leer

ointment

(noun) An ointment is a smooth thick substance that you put on sore skin to heal it.
e.g. *applying antibiotic cream or ointment.*
balm cream embrocation liniment lotion salve

okay

(adjective; an informal word) Okay means all right.

e.g. *Tell me if this sounds okay.*

acceptable adequate not bad passable satisfactory so-so tolerable

old

(adjective) having lived or existed for a long time.

e.g. *old clothes.*

aged age-old ancient antiquated antique dated decrepit elderly grey mature senile venerable worn-out

old-fashioned

(adjective) Something which is old-fashioned is no longer fashionable.

e.g. *old-fashioned shoes.*

ancient antiquated archaic bygone dated dead obsolete outmoded passé past

omen

(noun) An omen is something that is thought to be a sign of what will happen in the future.

e.g. *John saw this success as a good omen for his trip to Luxembourg.*

indication portent sign

ominous

(adjective) suggesting that something unpleasant is going to happen.

e.g. *an ominous sign.*

dark forbidding menacing sinister threatening unfavourable

opening

1. (noun) An opening is a hole or gap.

e.g. *A small opening is left at the top.*

aperture breach break cleft crack gap hole mouth

orifice space

2. An opening is also an opportunity.

e.g. *an opening in show business.*

chance occasion opportunity place vacancy

opinion

(noun) An opinion is a belief or view.

e.g. *The general opinion was that war would not come.*

belief estimation feeling idea judgment view

opposite

(noun) If two things are completely different, they are opposites.

e.g. *Whatever you think their response will be you can expect to hear the opposite.*

antithesis contradiction contrary contrast converse inverse reverse

oppress

(verb) To oppress people means to treat them cruelly or unfairly.

e.g. *resolved to raise issues that specifically oppress women.*

afflict burden crush harass harry persecute subjugate tyrannize

oral

(adjective) spoken rather than written.

e.g. *oral history.*

spoken verbal vocal

ordeal

(noun) An ordeal is a difficult and extremely unpleasant experience.

e.g. *the ordeal of being arrested and charged with attempted murder.*

affliction agony hardship nightmare suffering trial tribulation

order

1. (noun) An order is a command.

e.g. *Quickly she gave her orders.*

command decree dictate direction directive injunction instruction

2. If things are done in a particular order, they are done in that sequence.

e.g. *in alphabetical order.*

arrangement array grouping layout pattern plan sequence

orderly

(adjective) Something that is orderly is well organized or arranged.

e.g. *the children standing in an orderly line behind their father.*

businesslike controlled decorous disciplined methodical neat regular shipshape systematic tidy

ordinary

(adjective) Ordinary means not special or different in any way.

e.g. *I'm wearing an ordinary shirt and slacks.*

average common commonplace conventional customary everyday familiar household mundane normal pedestrian regular routine standard stock typical usual workaday

organization

(noun) An organization is any group, society, club, or business.

e.g. *Lie low - don't join any student body or organization.*

association body company concern consortium corporation group grouping league network syndicate

origin

(noun) You can refer to the beginning or cause of something as its origin or origins.

e.g. *traces of its nineteenth century origins.*

beginning birth dawning derivation emergence foundation genesis roots source

outline

(noun) The outline of something is its shape.

e.g. *the vague outline of the distant mountains.*

contour form profile shape silhouette

overjoyed

(adjective) extremely pleased.

e.g. *Francis was overjoyed to see him.*

delighted elated joyful jubilant rapturous thrilled

overrule

(verb) To overrule a person or their decisions means to decide that their decisions are incorrect.

e.g. *The Home Secretary refused to overrule the decision.*

annul cancel countermand invalidate override rescind reverse revoke veto

own

(verb) If you own something, it belongs to you.

e.g. *Sam owned a chain of liquor stores.*

enjoy have hold keep possess retain

P p

pacify

(verb) If you pacify someone who is angry, you calm them.
e.g. *The chairman was trying to pacify the audience.*
appease conciliate mollify placate soothe

pain

(noun) Pain is an unpleasant feeling of physical hurt or deep unhappiness.
e.g. *a sharp, stabbing pain.*
ache hurt pang smart sting suffering tenderness torment twinge

paltry

(adjective) If something is paltry, it is very small or insignificant.
e.g. *a paltry contribution.*
beggarly contemptible derisory insignificant miserable sorry trifling wretched

paper

(noun) A paper is an article on a particular subject presented at a conference or in a journal.
e.g. *supervisors adding their names to a paper without contributing to the work.*
article dissertation report thesis treatise

paralyse

(verb) If something paralyses you, it causes loss of feeling and movement in your body.
e.g. *a poison dart designed to paralyse its victim.*
freeze immobilize incapacitate numb petrify transfix

paraphrase

(verb) If you paraphrase what someone has said, you express it in a different way.

e.g. *He paraphrased my comments about the course.*

interpret rephrase restate reword

pardonable

(adjective) If you describe someone's bad behaviour as pardonable, you mean that you understand why they did it and think that they should be forgiven.

e.g. *This was an exaggeration, but a pardonable one.*

excusable forgivable understandable venial

parody

(noun) A parody is an amusing imitation of the style of an author or of a familiar situation.

e.g. *It was intended as a parody of a chat show.*

burlesque caricature imitation lampoon satire skit spoof takeoff travesty

part

(noun) A part of something is one of the pieces, sections, or aspects that it consists of.

e.g. *a new six-part TV series.*

aspect bit component constituent element fragment member piece section

participate

(verb) If you participate in an activity, you take part in it.

e.g. *The audience will be encouraged to participate.*

engage in join in partake share take part

pass

1. (verb) To pass something means to move past it.

e.g. *I pass a bakery on the way to work every day.*

go by *or* past move past

2. When a period of time passes, it happens and finishes.

e.g. *You're having a bad time just now, but it will pass.*

elapse go by lapse

passing

(adjective) lasting only for a short time.

e.g. *a passing phase.*

brief ephemeral fleeting momentary short-lived temporary transient transitory

passion

(noun) Passion is a very strong feeling, especially of sexual attraction.

e.g. *There's no passion at all in their marriage.*

ardour fervour fire force intensity lust rapture vehemence warmth

passionate

(adjective) expressing very strong feelings about something.

e.g. *his deep knowledge and passionate love of his subject.*

amorous ardent fervent fiery frenzied hot-blooded impassioned intense vehement warm wild

passive

(adjective) remaining calm and showing no feeling when provoked.

e.g. *Women are brought up to think of themselves as passive and weak.*

compliant inactive inert quiescent submissive

pastime

(noun) A pastime is a hobby or something you do just for pleasure.

e.g. *His favourite pastime is golf.*

activity hobby interest pursuit recreation

pathetic

(adjective) weak, inadequate, or helpless.

e.g. *the most pathetic and heart-rending story of the war.*

affecting forlorn moving pitiable pitiful plaintive poignant sorry touching

patience

(noun) Patience is the ability to stay calm in a difficult or irritating situation.

e.g. *No man's patience is infinite.*

forbearance restraint stoicism tolerance

pay

(verb) When you pay money to someone, you give it to them because you are buying something or owe it to them.

e.g. *Lewis didn't offer to pay for any of it.*

recompense reimburse settle square up

peace

(noun) Peace is a state of undisturbed calm and quiet.

e.g. *I will never forget the peace of that summer morning.*

calm concord harmony quiet repose serenity tranquillity

peaceful

(adjective) quiet, calm, and free from disturbance.

e.g. *a small luxurious hotel in peaceful surroundings.*

calm harmonious placid quiet restful serene tranquil

peak

(noun) The peak of an activity or process is the point at which it is strongest or most successful.

e.g. *He's at the peak of his career.*

acme apex climax culmination height pinnacle summit zenith

peeved

(adjective; an informal word) irritated and annoyed.

e.g. *She looked a little peeved at being left out.*

annoyed exasperated irked irritated piqued put out riled sore vexed

peevish

(adjective) irritable and complaining.

e.g. *He looked surprised at my peevish retort.*

cantankerous complaining fractious fretful petulant plaintive querulous

pensive

(adjective) deep in thought.

e.g. *Patterson was in a particularly pensive mood.*

contemplative dreamy meditative preoccupied reflective thoughtful

pent-up

(adjective) Pent-up emotions have been held back for a long time without release.

e.g. *giving vent to her pent-up feelings.*

bottled-up repressed smothered stifled suppressed

people

1. (plural noun) People are men, women, and children.

e.g. *They murdered hundreds of people.*

folk human beings humanity mortals persons

2. (noun) A people is all the men, women, and children of a particular country or race.

e.g. *the peace and harmony on which the welfare of a people depends.*

citizens nation populace population public race

perceive

(verb) If you perceive something that is not obvious, you see it or realize it.

e.g. *I began to perceive the advantages of this arrangement.*
discern distinguish make out note notice observe remark spot

perceptive

(adjective) Someone who is perceptive realizes or notices things that are not obvious.

e.g. *an intelligent and perceptive man.*
acute astute discerning observant penetrating percipient perspicacious

perfect

1. (adjective) of the highest standard and without fault.

e.g. *His English was perfect.*
consummate faultless flawless ideal immaculate impeccable

2. (verb) If you perfect something, you make it as good as it can possibly be.

e.g. *Engineers were working to perfect a rocket.*
hone polish refine

permeate

(verb) To permeate something means to spread through it and affect every part of it.

e.g. *The feeling of failure permeates everything I do.*
impregnate penetrate percolate pervade seep suffuse

permissible

(adjective) allowed by the rules.

e.g. *restraints on what is permissible for publication.*
admissible allowable authorized legitimate permitted proper sanctioned

permission

(noun) If you have permission to do something, you are allowed to do it.

e.g. *There is no possibility of getting planning permission.*
authorization clearance consent dispensation go-ahead leave licence sanction

permit

(verb) To permit something means to allow it or make it possible.
e.g. *His wife would not permit an autopsy.*
allow authorize entitle grant let license sanction

persecute

(verb) To persecute someone means to treat them with continual cruelty and unfairness.
e.g. *We do not want to persecute minority groups.*
badger bait hound oppress pick on pursue torment victimize

persevere

(verb) If you persevere, you keep trying to do something and do not give up.
e.g. *He is determined to persevere with his medical studies.*
carry on continue go on keep going persist stick at

person

(noun) A person is a man, woman, or child.
e.g. *I'm not at all a violent person.*
character human human being individual soul

personal

(adjective) Personal means belonging or relating to a particular person rather than to people in general.
e.g. *my personal feeling.*
exclusive individual own particular private

persuade

(verb) If someone persuades you to do something or persuades you that something is true, they make you do it or believe it by giving you very good reasons.

e.g. *Do ads persuade you to buy a certain product?*

coax convince entice get induce prevail upon win over

perverted

(adjective) Someone who is perverted has disgusting or unacceptable behaviour or ideas, especially sexual behaviour or ideas.

e.g. *the product of a sick and perverted mind.*

abnormal deviant kinky sick twisted unnatural warped

pester

(verb) If you pester someone, you keep bothering them or asking them to do something.

e.g. *The kids have been pestering me to buy them new trainers.*

badger bother get at harass hassle importune nag plague torment worry

picture

(noun) A picture of someone or something is a drawing, painting, or photograph of them.

e.g. *a big picture on the front page.*

figure illustration impression likeness sketch

pierce

(verb) If a sharp object pierces something, it goes through it, making a hole.

e.g. *artillery powerful enough to pierce an armoured vehicle.*

penetrate perforate prick puncture stab transfix

piercing

(adjective) A piercing sound is high-pitched, sharp, and unpleasant.

e.g. *She let out a piercing wail.*

ear-splitting excruciating high-pitched penetrating sharp shrill

pity

1. (verb) If you pity someone, you feel very sorry for them.

e.g. *I pity the poor man she marries.*

commiserate with feel for feel sorry for grieve for have compassion for sympathize with

2. (noun) Pity is a feeling of being sorry for someone.

e.g. *He felt, instead, a flash of pity and a desire to put things right.*

commiseration compassion fellow feeling sympathy

place

(noun) A place is any point, building, or area.

e.g. *a public place.*

area location point position site situation spot whereabouts

placid

(adjective) calm and not easily excited or upset.

e.g. *Labradors are usually placid dogs.*

calm equable even-tempered phlegmatic tranquil unruffled

plain

1. (adjective) very simple in style with no pattern or decoration.

e.g. *plain walls.*

austere bare basic natural restrained severe simple stark unadorned

2. obvious and easy to understand or recognize.

e.g. *The facts are plain enough.*

apparent clear comprehensible distinct evident manifest obvious patent transparent unambiguous unmistakable visible

plan

1. (noun) A plan is a method of achieving something that has been worked out beforehand.

e.g. *a long-term plan of action.*

blueprint design formula idea method policy procedure ruse scheme strategy system

2. (verb) If you plan something, you decide in detail what it is to be and how to do it.

e.g. *Plan your menu well in advance.*

arrange design devise draft formulate organize

3. If you are planning to do something, you intend to do it.

e.g. *They plan to marry in the summer.*

aim intend mean propose

pleasant

(adjective) enjoyable, likable, or attractive.

e.g. *a pleasant personality.*

agreeable amiable charming congenial delectable delightful engaging enjoyable good gracious gratifying likable nice personable pleasing pleasurable

please

(verb) If something pleases you, it makes you feel happy and satisfied.

e.g. *He's very easy to please.*

cheer content delight gladden gratify satisfy suit tickle

pliable

(adjective) If something is pliable, you can bend it without breaking it.

e.g. *pliable stems.*

ductile elastic flexible malleable plastic pliant supple

plot

1. (noun) A plot is a secret plan made by a group of people.

e.g. *the potential victim of some plot.*

conspiracy intrigue stratagem subterfuge

2. (verb) If people plot to do something, they plan it secretly.

e.g. *His family is plotting to disinherit him.*

conspire manoeuvre scheme

plump

(adjective) rather fat.

e.g. *a small plump baby.*

buxom chubby dumpy podgy portly roly-poly stout tubby

plunge

(verb) If something plunges, it falls suddenly.

e.g. *He plunged into the cold sea.*

dive drop fall pitch plummet sink swoop

poison

(noun) Poison is a substance that can kill people or animals if they swallow it or absorb it.

e.g. *He tried to kill his wife with rat poison.*

toxin venom

poke

(verb) If you poke someone or something, you push at them quickly with your finger or a sharp object.

e.g. *He poked me in the eye with his finger.*

dig jab prod stab

polish

(verb) If you polish something, you put polish on it or rub it with a cloth to make it shine.

e.g. *Every Sunday he polishes his car.*

buff burnish rub shine wax

polite

(adjective) Someone who is polite has good manners and behaves considerately towards other people.

e.g. *It doesn't cost anything to be polite.*

civil courteous gracious respectful well-behaved well-mannered

pollute

(verb) To pollute water or air means to make it dirty and dangerous to use or live in.

e.g. *These gases pollute the atmosphere.*

contaminate dirty foul infect mar poison sully taint

ponder

(verb) If you ponder, you think about something deeply.

e.g. *He was pondering the problem when Phillipson drove up.*

brood over cogitate contemplate deliberate meditate mull over muse reflect ruminate

pontificate

(verb) If someone pontificates, they state their opinions as if they are obviously correct.

e.g. *He loves to pontificate on things he knows nothing about.*

expound hold forth lay down the law

poor

(adjective) Poor people have very little money and few possessions.

e.g. *She came from a very poor family.*

destitute impecunious impoverished needy penniless penurious poverty-stricken

popular

(adjective) enjoyed, approved of, or liked by a lot of people.

e.g. *a very popular family car.*

fashionable favourite in in favour prevailing well-liked

portion

(noun) A portion of something is a part or amount of it.

e.g. *a portion of fresh fruit.*

helping piece share

pose

(noun) A pose is the way someone is sitting, standing, or lying.

e.g. *hundreds of photographs in various poses.*

attitude position posture stance

positive

(adjective) providing definite proof of the truth or identity of something.

e.g. *positive evidence.*

affirmative categorical certain clear-cut conclusive concrete decisive definite explicit firm unmistakable

possession

(noun) Your possessions are the things that you own or that you have with you.

e.g. *I came home to find Billy rooting through my possessions.*

assets belongings chattels effects property things

possibility

(noun) A possibility is something that might be true or might happen.

e.g. *the possibility of a ban.*

chance hope likelihood prospect

possible

(adjective) likely to happen or able to be done.

e.g. *They want to raise as much money for charity as possible.*

conceivable feasible potential practicable

postpone

(verb) If you postpone an event, you arrange for it to take place at a later time than was originally planned.

e.g. *We'll have to postpone our meeting.*

adjourn defer procrastinate put off shelve

potential

(adjective) capable of becoming the kind of thing mentioned.

e.g. *potential sources of finance.*

dormant future latent likely possible unrealized

pour

(verb) When it is raining heavily, you can say that it is pouring.

e.g. *It was the rush hour and pouring with rain.*

bucket pelt teem

poverty

(noun) Poverty is the state of being very poor.

e.g. *conditions of dire poverty.*

destitution need penury privation want

power

(noun) The power of something is the physical strength that it has to move things.

e.g. *The car handled nicely but lacked power.*

energy force potency strength

powerless

(adjective) unable to control or influence events.

e.g. *She was powerless to save her son.*

helpless impotent incapable

practical

(adjective) Ideas, methods, tools, or clothes that are practical are sensible and likely to be effective.

e.g. *practical low-heeled shoes.*

businesslike down-to-earth functional pragmatic realistic sensible utilitarian

praise

1. (verb) If you praise someone or something, you express strong approval of their qualities or achievements.

e.g. *It is important to praise children when they do well.*

acclaim applaud commend compliment congratulate eulogize extol

2. (noun) Praise is what is said or written in approval of someone's qualities or achievements.

e.g. *I don't deserve half of your generous praise.*

acclamation accolade applause approval commendation compliment congratulation eulogy tribute

precarious

1. (adjective) If your situation is precarious, you may fail in what you are doing at any time.

e.g. *Advertising is a precarious profession.*

dangerous dicey *informal* dodgy *informal* doubtful hairy *informal* hazardous risky uncertain

2. Something that is precarious is likely to fall because it is not well balanced or secured.

e.g. *precarious-looking iron bridges.*

insecure shaky unsafe unstable unsteady

precaution

(noun) A precaution is an action that is intended to prevent something from happening.

e.g. *It's still worth taking precautions against accidents.*

insurance safeguard safety measure

predicament

(noun) If you are in a predicament, you are in a difficult situation.

e.g. *the hopelessness of her predicament.*

corner dilemma emergency fix *informal* hole *informal* plight quandary

predict

(verb) If someone predicts an event, they say that it will happen in the future.

e.g. *Observers predict a glittering future for him.*
forecast foresee foretell prophesy

predominant

(adjective) more important or more noticeable than anything else in a particular set of people or things.
e.g. *the predominant opinion in the West.*
controlling dominant main paramount prevailing prevalent principal ruling

preliminary

(adjective) Preliminary activities take place before something starts, in preparation for it.
e.g. *the preliminary rounds of the competition.*
introductory prefatory preparatory qualifying trial

premonition

(noun) A premonition is a feeling that something unpleasant is going to happen.
e.g. *a sudden premonition of disaster.*
apprehension foreboding presentiment

present

(adjective) A present situation is one that exists now rather than in the past or the future.
e.g. *How satisfied are you with your present job?*
contemporary current existing immediate present-day

prestige

(noun) If you have prestige, people admire you because of your position.
e.g. *a position of wealth and prestige.*
distinction eminence esteem renown standing stature status

presume

(verb) If you presume something, you think that it is the case although you have no proof.

e.g. *I presume the vacancy will be advertised.*

assume presuppose suppose surmise

pretend

(verb) If you pretend that something is the case, you try to make people believe that it is, although in fact it is not.

e.g. *Latimer pretended not to notice.*

affect bluff feign profess sham simulate

prevent

(verb) If you prevent something, you stop it from happening or being done.

e.g. *efforts to prevent publication.*

avert avoid balk foil forestall frustrate preclude restrain stave off stop

previous

(adjective) happening or existing before something else in time or position.

e.g. *previous reports.*

earlier former old past preceding prior

price

(noun) The price of something is the amount of money you have to pay to buy it.

e.g. *two for the price of one.*

amount charge cost fee figure rate

pride

(noun) Pride is a feeling of satisfaction you have when you have done something well.

e.g. *He can look back on his efforts with pride.*

dignity honour satisfaction self-esteem self-respect

prim

(adjective) Someone who is prim always behaves very correctly and is easily shocked by anything rude.

e.g. *She acts like a prim maiden aunt.*

priggish proper prudish puritanical staid strait-laced

prime

(noun) Someone's prime is the stage when they are at their strongest, most active, or most successful.

e.g. *I'm not middle-aged, I'm in my prime.*

best bloom height heyday

principle

(noun) A principle is a belief you have about the way you should behave.

e.g. *I try to live according to my principles.*

belief ethic ideal moral standard value

prize

(noun) A prize is a reward given to the winner of a competition or game.

e.g. *the star prize in the raffle.*

award jackpot reward trophy winnings

probability

(noun) The probability of something happening is how likely it is to happen.

e.g. *This will greatly increase the probability of success.*

chance expectation likelihood odds prospect

problem

(noun) A problem is an unsatisfactory situation that causes difficulties.

e.g. *The problem is reaching epidemic proportions.*

complication difficulty drawback hitch snag

productive

1. (adjective) To be productive means to produce a large number of things.

e.g. *Farms were more productive in these areas.*

fertile fruitful prolific

2. If something such as a meeting is productive, good or useful things happen as a result of it.

e.g. *a long and productive life.*

fruitful profitable rewarding useful worthwhile

profit

(noun) When someone sells something, the profit is the amount they gain by selling it for more than it cost them to buy or make.

e.g. *We split the profit between us.*

earnings gains proceeds receipts returns revenue takings

programme

(noun) You can refer to a planned series of events as a programme.

e.g. *her packed programme of official engagements.*

agenda course curriculum schedule syllabus timetable

progress

1. (noun) Progress is the process of gradually improving or getting near to achieving something.

e.g. *They made good progress.*

advance development headway improvement

2. The progress of something is the way in which it develops or continues.

e.g. *news on the progress of the war.*

course development movement progression

promiscuous

(adjective) Someone who is promiscuous has sex with many

different people.

e.g. *You don't have to be promiscuous to be at risk from AIDS.*

abandoned debauched dissipated dissolute licentious loose wanton

promise

1. (verb) If you promise to do something, you say that you will definitely do it.

e.g. *He would never promise something he couldn't fulfil.*

guarantee pledge swear undertake vow

2. (noun) A promise is a statement made by someone that they will definitely do something.

e.g. *He made a promise to the men.*

assurance oath pledge vow word

prone

(adjective) If you are prone to something, you have a tendency to be affected by it or to do it.

e.g. *She is prone to depression.*

disposed given inclined liable predisposed subject susceptible

proof

(noun) If you have proof of something, you have evidence which shows that it happened, is true, or exists.

e.g. *Here's proof that this idea works.*

authentication confirmation corroboration evidence substantiation verification

prospect

(noun) Someone's prospects are their chances of being successful in the future.

e.g. *I wanted to further my career prospects.*

expectation future outlook

proud

(adjective) having great dignity and self-respect.

e.g. *He was too proud to ask his family for help.*

arrogant conceited haughty high and mighty *informal* self-important snooty *informal* stuck-up *informal*

prove

(verb) To prove that something is true means to provide evidence that it is definitely true.

e.g. *A letter from Nora proved that he lived there.*

authenticate confirm corroborate demonstrate establish show substantiate verify

provide

(verb) If you provide something for someone, you give it to them or make it available for them.

e.g. *a network of friends who can provide help and support.*

cater for equip furnish lay on purvey stock up supply

public

(adjective) provided for everyone to use, or open to anyone.

e.g. *public transport.*

civic civil communal general national open state unrestricted

punctual

(adjective) arriving at the correct time.

e.g. *He dislikes people who are not punctual.*

on time prompt timely

punish

(verb) To punish someone who has done something wrong means to make them suffer because of it.

e.g. *You've got to punish the ringleaders.*

chastise correct discipline penalize

pure

1. (adjective) Pure means clean and free from harmful substances.

e.g. *The water is pure enough to drink.*

clean spotless sterile sterilized unadulterated unpolluted unsullied

2. People who are pure have not done anything considered to be sinful.

e.g. *a pure young woman of good family.*

blameless chaste impeccable innocent undefiled unsullied virginal virtuous

push

(verb) When you push something, you press it using force in order to move it.

e.g. *Push the table back against the wall.*

drive jog jostle poke press propel ram shove thrust

put

(verb) When you put something somewhere, you move it into that place or position.

e.g. *He sat back and put his feet on the desk.*

deposit fix lay place position rest set settle

put across

(verb) When you put something across, you make someone understand it.

e.g. *It's very hard to put across the facts.*

communicate convey explain spell out

puzzle

(verb) If something puzzles you, it confuses you and you do not understand it.

e.g. *There was something about her that puzzled me.*

baffle bamboozle bemuse bewilder confound confuse flummox mystify perplex stump

Q q

quarrel

1. (noun) A quarrel is an angry argument.

e.g. *I had a terrible quarrel with my other brothers.*

altercation argument disagreement dispute fight row squabble tiff

2. (verb) If people quarrel, they have an angry argument.

e.g. *The man quarrelled with the driver.*

argue bicker differ disagree dispute fall out fight row squabble wrangle

quarrelsome

(adjective) often quarrelling.

e.g. *His brothers were greedy and quarrelsome.*

argumentative contentious

question

1. (noun) A question is a sentence which asks for information.

e.g. *You haven't answered my question.*

inquiry query

2. (verb) If you question something, you express doubts about it.

e.g. *He never stopped questioning his own beliefs.*

challenge dispute query

quiet

(adjective) Someone or something that is quiet makes very little noise or no noise at all.

e.g. *that quiet manner of his.*

hushed inaudible low silent soft soundless subdued unobtrusive

quote

1. (verb) If you quote a fact, you state it because it supports what you are saying.

e.g. *She quoted a great line from a book.*

cite detail instance name recite

2. (noun) A quote is an extract from a book or speech.

e.g. *a quote from the newspaper.*

citation quotation

R r

rage

(verb) To rage about something means to speak angrily about it.
e.g. *He raged about the unfairness of this.*
fume rant rave seethe storm

rampage

(verb) To rampage means to rush about wildly causing damage.
e.g. *Within minutes the mob was rampaging through the streets.*
go berserk rage run amuck run riot storm

ramshackle

(adjective) A ramshackle building is in poor condition, and likely to fall down.
e.g. *a ramshackle old tractor shed.*
crumbling decrepit derelict dilapidated rickety tumbledown

random

(adjective) A random choice or arrangement is not based on any definite plan.
e.g. *a random sample of local residents.*
arbitrary chance fortuitous haphazard unplanned

range

(noun) A range is a number of different things of the same kind.
e.g. *A wide range of colours are available.*
extent gamut scope spectrum sweep variety

rapport

(noun; a formal word) If there is a rapport between two people, they find it easy to understand each other's feelings and attitudes.

e.g. *The emotional rapport between mother and child.*

affinity bond empathy harmony sympathy understanding

rash

(adjective) If you are rash, you do something hasty and foolish.

e.g. *It would be a rash pundit who would bet against him.*

foolhardy hasty heedless hot-headed ill-advised impetuous imprudent impulsive incautious irresponsible reckless

rather

1. (adverb) Rather means to a certain extent.

e.g. *The reality is rather complex.*

fairly moderately quite relatively slightly somewhat

2. If you would rather do a particular thing, you would prefer to do it.

e.g. *I would rather stay here.*

preferably sooner

ratio

(noun) A ratio is a relationship which shows how many times one thing is bigger than another.

e.g. *The adult to child ratio is 1 to 6.*

proportion rate relation

reaction

1. (noun) Your reaction to something is what you feel, say, or do because of it.

e.g. *Reaction to the visit is mixed.*

feedback response

2. If there is a reaction against something, it becomes unpopular.

e.g. *a reaction against Christianity.*

backlash

real

(adjective) genuine and not imitation.

e.g. *Who's to know if they're real guns?*

actual authentic genuine original

reality

(noun) Reality is the real nature of things, rather than the way someone imagines it.

e.g. *Fiction and reality were increasingly blurred.*

actuality fact facts truth

reason

1. (noun) The reason for something is the fact or situation which explains why it happens or which causes it to happen.

e.g. *Most women cite self-defence as their reason for carrying a gun.*

cause grounds motive

2. Reason is the ability to think and make judgments.

e.g. *He lost all sense of reason.*

intellect judgment logic sense understanding

rebellion

(noun) A rebellion is organized and often violent opposition to authority.

e.g. *a ferocious rebellion against Russian settlers.*

insurrection mutiny resistance revolt revolution uprising

recession

(noun) A recession is a period when a country's economy is less successful and more people become unemployed.

e.g. *The recession has damaged the chances of disabled people obtaining work.*

decline depression downturn slump

recognize

(verb) If you recognize someone or something, you realize that you know who or what they are.

e.g. *The receptionist recognized me at once.*
identify know place remember

reconstruct

1. (verb) To reconstruct something that has been damaged means to build it again.
e.g. *The dilapidated house was to have been reconstructed brick by brick.*
rebuild renovate restore

2. To reconstruct a past event means to obtain a complete description of it from small pieces of information.
e.g. *Hutchinson later reconstructed the alleged murder for police.*
build up recreate regenerate

record

1. (noun) If you keep a record of something, you keep a written account or store information in a computer.
e.g. *medical records.*
annals archive chronicle file history minutes

2. (verb) If you record information, you write it down or put it into a computer.
e.g. *The coroner recorded a verdict of accidental death.*
enter file log minute register report transcribe

recover

1. (verb) To recover from an illness or unhappy experience means to get well again or get over it.
e.g. *He was recovering from a serious head injury.*
convalesce heal improve mend rally recuperate revive

2. If you recover a lost object or your ability to do something, you get it back.
e.g. *Harry recovered his sense of humour.*
make good reclaim recoup regain repossess retrieve

reduce

(verb) To reduce something means to make it smaller in size or amount.

e.g. *Cuts have severely reduced the number of schools with their own orchestras.*

compress condense curtail cut decrease diminish dock lessen lower narrow pare shorten trim

refined

(adjective) very polite and well-mannered.

e.g. *Football is meant to be a refined and cultured art.*

civilized cultivated cultured genteel ladylike polished polite urbane

reform

(verb) When people reform, they stop committing crimes or doing other unacceptable things.

e.g. *When his first court case was coming up, James promised to reform.*

go straight mend your ways turn over a new leaf

refresh

(verb) If something refreshes you when you are hot or tired, it makes you feel cooler or more energetic.

e.g. *a refreshing glass of fruit juice.*

freshen invigorate revitalize revive stimulate

refuge

(noun) A refuge is a place where you go for safety.

e.g. *The pink-walled cottage was his refuge from the bustle of London.*

asylum haven retreat sanctuary shelter

refund

(verb) To refund someone's money means to return it to them after they have paid for something with it.

e.g. *The seller of the dog is legally bound to refund your money.*

pay back reimburse repay

region

(noun) A region is a large area of land.

e.g. *He went to live in a remote region of Spain.*

area district expanse province sector territory zone

regret

(verb) If you regret something, you are sorry that it happened.

e.g. *I do regret not having had a proper education.*

bemoan deplore mourn repent rue

regular

(adjective) even and equally spaced.

e.g. *soft music with a regular beat.*

consistent constant even fixed set steady symmetrical uniform

reject

1. (verb) If you reject a proposal or request, you do not accept it or agree to it.

e.g. *The Rugby League rejected their appeal for compensation.*

decline rebuff refuse repudiate turn down

2. If you reject a belief, political system, or way of life, you decide that it is not for you.

e.g. *Some adolescents reject the lifestyle of the older generation.*

discard renounce repudiate shun spurn

relation

(noun) If there is a relation between two things, they are similar or connected in some way.

e.g. *This theory bears no relation to reality.*

comparison connection correspondence relationship similarity

relax

1. (verb) If you relax, you become calm and your muscles lose their tension.

e.g. *We can all relax over coffee and biscuits.*
loosen up rest unwind

2. If you relax your hold, you hold something less tightly.
e.g. *The German relaxed his grip on the steering wheel.*
ease loose loosen slacken weaken

relegate

(verb) To relegate something or someone means to give them a less important position or status.
e.g. *He was relegated to the role of spectator.*
demote downgrade

relentless

(adjective) never stopping and never reducing in severity.
e.g. *the relentless rise of business closures.*
pitiless remorseless uncompromising unrelenting unyielding

relevant

(adjective) If something is relevant, it is connected with and is appropriate to what is being discussed.
e.g. *We have passed all relevant information on to the police.*
applicable apposite appropriate germane pertinent related

religion

(noun) A religion is a system of religious belief.
e.g. *Every religion has elements that can offend people of a different faith.*
creed cult sect

religious

(adjective) Someone who is religious has a strong belief in a god or gods.
e.g. *A kind-hearted and deeply religious woman.*
devout godly pious

remains

(plural noun) The remains of something are the parts that are left after most of it has been destroyed.

e.g. *the remains of an ancient mosque.*

debris remnants traces vestiges

remark

1. (verb) If you remark on something, you mention it or comment on it.

e.g. *On several occasions she had remarked on the boy's improvement.*

comment mention

2. (noun) A remark is something you say, often in a casual way.

e.g. *He made some banal remark about the lateness of the spring.*

comment observation utterance

remarkable

(adjective) impressive and unexpected.

e.g. *It was a remarkable achievement.*

impressive notable noteworthy outstanding phenomenal significant singular striking uncommon wonderful

remember

(verb) If you can remember someone or something from the past, you can bring them into your mind or think about them.

e.g. *I can still remember the headlines on the newspaper placards.*

commemorate recall recognize recollect reminisce

remorse

(noun; a formal word) Remorse is a strong feeling of guilt.

e.g. *Keith spent the night in sleepless remorse at what he had done.*

compunction contrition penitence regret repentance self-reproach

remove

(verb) If you remove something from a place, you take it off or away.

e.g. *He removed the stereo from his brother's car.*

detach efface eject eliminate extract obviate oust purge weed out withdraw

repel

(verb) When soldiers repel an attacking force, they successfully defend themselves against it.

e.g. *Desperate operations to repel the Japanese invasion of New Guinea.*

parry repulse resist ward off

replace

(verb) When one thing replaces another, the first thing takes the place of the second.

e.g. *John Roberts yesterday replaced Jeremy Beasley as chairman.*

oust succeed supersede supplant

reply

1. (verb) If you reply to something, you say or write an answer.

e.g. *a polite refusal to reply.*

answer respond retaliate retort return riposte write back

2. (noun) A reply is what you say or write when you answer someone.

e.g. *They never received a reply.*

answer comeback *informal* rejoinder response retort return riposte

report

(noun) A report is an account of an event, a situation, or a person's progress.

e.g. *Your report about banking errors was most enlightening.*

account article description piece statement story write-up

represent

(verb) To represent something in a particular way means to describe it in that way.

e.g. *The popular press tends to represent him as a hero.*

depict describe portray render show

representation

(noun) You can describe a picture or statue of someone as a representation of them.

e.g. *The photograph was not an accurate representation of the star.*

likeness portrait portrayal profile

reputation

(noun) The reputation of something or someone is the opinion that people have of them.

e.g. *The college had a good reputation.*

character honour name repute standing

request

(noun) If you make a request for something, you ask for it politely and formally.

e.g. *She turned down my request for an interview.*

appeal application entreaty petition

resemblance

(noun) If there is a resemblance between two things, they are similar to each other.

e.g. *There was a remarkable resemblance between him and Pete.*

correspondence likeness similarity

reserve

(verb) If something is reserved for a particular person or purpose, it is kept specially for them.

e.g. *a wing of the prison reserved for foreigners.*

book earmark keep preserve save set aside

resist

(verb) If you resist something, you refuse to accept it and try to prevent it.

e.g. *The pay squeeze will be fiercely resisted by the unions.*

combat dispute oppose withstand

resonant

(adjective) A resonant sound is deep and strong.

e.g. *His voice was resonant and beautifully cultured.*

echoing full resounding reverberating rich sonorous

respectable

1. (adjective) considered to be acceptable and morally correct.

e.g. *the veneer of respectable society.*

decent decorous honourable proper reputable respected upright worthy

2. adequate or reasonable.

e.g. *a respectable final score.*

adequate ample appreciable considerable decent fair presentable reasonable substantial

responsibility

(noun) If you accept responsibility for something that has happened, you agree that you caused it or were to blame.

e.g. *They refuse to accept responsibility for the children.*

blame liability obligation onus

responsible

(adjective) If you are responsible for something, it is your duty to deal with it and you are to blame if it goes wrong.

e.g. *The airline was responsible for the safety of the passengers.*

accountable answerable liable

rest

(noun) If you have a rest, you sit or lie quietly and relax.

e.g. *He had gone on the trip with his wife for a well-earned rest.*

break breather lull respite stop time off

restless

(adjective) finding it difficult to remain still or relaxed as a result of boredom or impatience.

e.g. *bored and restless youths.*

agitated disturbed edgy fidgety jumpy restive uneasy unsettled

restore

(verb) To restore an old building or work of art means to clean and repair it.

e.g. *She restored the old fort and made it into her private temple.*

do up refurbish renovate retouch

restrain

(verb) To restrain someone or something means to hold them back or prevent them from doing what they want to.

e.g. *Manning had to be restrained from leaping overboard.*

check contain control curb hold back inhibit suppress

restrict

(verb) To restrict people or animals means to limit their movement or actions.

e.g. *Visibility may be restricted by fog.*

confine cramp hem in impede inhibit limit restrain

restriction

(noun) A restriction is a rule or situation that limits what you can do.

e.g. *financial restrictions.*

check condition constraint control limitation restraint

result

(noun) The result of something is the situation that is caused by it.

e.g. *As a result of the incident he got a two-year suspension.*
aftereffect aftermath consequence effect outcome repercussion upshot

retract

(verb) If you retract something you have said, you say that you did not mean it.

e.g. *He retracted his confession.*
recant renege repudiate revoke take back withdraw

reveal

(verb) To reveal something means to tell people about it.

e.g. *They were not ready to reveal any of the details.*
disclose divulge impart leak let slip publish tell unfold unveil

revel

(verb) If you revel in a situation, you enjoy it very much.

e.g. *She revelled in her stardom.*
delight luxuriate relish savour thrive on wallow

revenge

1. (noun) Revenge involves hurting someone who has hurt you.

e.g. *She wanted to get her revenge on her brother.*
reprisal retaliation retribution vengeance

2. (verb) If you revenge yourself on someone who has hurt you, you hurt them in return.

e.g. *Nothing gave her greater pleasure than revenging herself on Buxton.*
avenge even the score retaliate vindicate

review

1. (noun) When there is a review of a situation or system, it is examined to decide whether changes are needed.

e.g. *an impartial review of education in Birmingham.*
evaluation examination reassessment

2. (verb) To review something means to examine it to decide whether changes are needed.
e.g. *The cabinet will meet this morning to review its economic policy.*
evaluate reassess reconsider rethink revise

rhythm

(noun) Rhythm is a regular movement or beat.
e.g. *He heard the rhythm of Markham's breathing change.*
beat cadence metre pulse tempo time

rich

(adjective) Someone who is rich has a lot of money and possessions.
e.g. *lifestyles of the rich and famous.*
affluent loaded *informal* prosperous wealthy
well-heeled *slang* well-off well-to-do

rid

(verb; a formal use) To rid a place of something unpleasant means to succeed in removing it.
e.g. *the campaign to rid football of racism.*
clear free purge relieve unburden

riddle

(noun) Something that is a riddle puzzles and confuses you.
e.g. *Scientists claimed to have solved the riddle of the birth of the Universe.*
conundrum enigma mystery poser puzzle

right

1. (adjective) The right choice, action, or decision is the best or most suitable one.
e.g. *I feel sure this is the right thing to do.*
equitable ethical fair fitting just proper suitable

2. (noun) If you have a right to do something, you are morally or legally entitled to do it.

e.g. *You have the right to appeal against the decision.*
claim licence prerogative privilege

rigid

(adjective) Rigid laws or systems cannot be changed and are considered severe.
e.g. *Examiners were supplied with a rigid marking scheme.*
inflexible rigorous strict unalterable uncompromising unyielding

ring

1. (verb) When a bell rings, it makes a clear, loud sound.
e.g. *The phone was ringing when I got home.*
chime clang knell peal toll

2. (noun) A ring is a small circle of metal worn on your finger.
e.g. *a wedding ring.*
band circle hoop

rise

(verb) If something rises, it moves upwards.
e.g. *Smoke rises up from the odd cottage chimney.*
ascend climb lift mount soar

risk

1. (noun) A risk is a chance that something unpleasant or dangerous might happen.
e.g. *the risk of a heart attack.*
chance danger gamble

2. (verb) If you risk something unpleasant, you do something knowing that the unpleasant thing might happen as a result.
e.g. *If he doesn't play, he risks losing his place in the team.*
chance endanger gamble hazard imperil jeopardize venture

rival

(noun) Your rival is the person you are competing with.

e.g. *He has come up against a worthy rival.*

adversary challenger competitor contender opponent

rivalry

(noun) Rivalry is active competition between people.

e.g. *An intense rivalry has broken out between teenage computer wizards.*

competition conflict contention opposition

romantic

1. (adjective) connected with sexual love.

e.g. *a burst of romantic passion.*

amorous lovey-dovey loving mushy *informal* passionate sentimental sloppy *informal* soppy *British informal*

2. A romantic person has ideas that are not realistic, for example about love or about ways of changing society.

e.g. *the romantic ideal of bringing peace and unity to a divided country.*

dreamy high-flown idealistic impractical starry-eyed unrealistic

rot

1. (verb) When food or wood rots, it decays and can no longer be used.

e.g. *The wooden huts on the site were rotting and leaking.*

decay decompose deteriorate moulder perish putrefy

2. (noun) Rot is the condition that affects things when they rot.

e.g. *The timber frame was not protected against rot.*

blight canker decay mould

rotten

1. (adjective) decayed and no longer of use.

e.g. *The room smelled of fried onions, rotten fruit, and burned cooking oil.*

bad corrupt decayed decaying decomposed

decomposing disintegrating mouldering mouldy perished putrescent putrid

2. (an informal use) of very poor quality.

e.g. *She was a rotten driver.*

awful bad deplorable dreadful lousy terrible

rough

1. (adjective) uneven and not smooth.

e.g. *the rough surface of the stone.*

broken bumpy craggy irregular jagged rocky stony uneven

2. showing the main features but not the details.

e.g. *a rough sketch.*

approximate basic crude cursory hasty imperfect incomplete quick rudimentary shapeless sketchy

3. without enough care or gentleness.

e.g. *complaints of rough handling.*

harsh loutish nasty rowdy severe sharp tough violent

4. If the sea is rough, there are large waves because of bad weather.

e.g. *a rough Channel crossing.*

choppy squally stormy turbulent

round

(adjective) Something round is shaped like a ball or a circle.

e.g. *a round hole in the floor.*

circular curved cylindrical globular rotund rounded spherical

row

(noun) A row of people or things is several of them arranged in a line.

e.g. *a row of houses.*

bank column file line queue rank sequence tier

rowdy

(adjective) rough and noisy.

e.g. *a gang of rowdy youths.*

disorderly noisy obstreperous rough stroppy *informal* unruly uproarious

royal

(adjective) belonging to or involving a queen, a king, or a member of their family.

e.g. *They built a royal palace for their king.*

august imperial princely queenly regal sovereign

rubbish

1. (noun) Rubbish is unwanted things or waste material.

e.g. *a filthy campsite covered in rubbish.*

debris garbage junk litter refuse trash waste

2. You can refer to nonsense or something of very poor quality as rubbish.

e.g. *Ferguson dismissed the claims as rubbish.*

drivel gibberish nonsense piffle *informal* rot trash twaddle

rude

(adjective) not polite.

e.g. *rude remarks about politicians.*

abusive discourteous impolite insolent insulting offhand uncivil unmannerly

rule

(noun) Rules are statements which tell you what you are allowed to do.

e.g. *the rules of grammar.*

axiom direction guideline law maxim order ordinance precept principle regulation standard

rumour

(noun) A rumour is a story that people are talking about, which may or may not be true.

e.g. *There was a rumour that two policemen had been shot.*

gossip hearsay report story whisper word

run

1. (verb) When you run, you move quickly, leaving the ground during each stride.

e.g. *I whooped for joy and ran across the lawn shouting.*

bolt career dart dash gallop hare hasten hurry jog race rush scamper scramble scurry speed sprint

2. If you run away from a place, you leave it suddenly and secretly.

e.g. *He ran away from his school.*

abscond bolt decamp escape flee go

runaway

(noun) A runaway is a person who has escaped from a place or left it secretly and hurriedly.

e.g. *They battled for three hours to catch the runaways.*

deserter escapee fugitive truant

rural

(adjective) relating to or involving the countryside.

e.g. *a deeply felt nostalgia for rural life.*

country pastoral rustic

S s

sack

(verb; an informal use) If someone is sacked, they are dismissed from their job by their employer.

e.g. *the tearful face of the maid she'd sacked for theft.*

discharge   dismiss   fire

sacrifice

(verb) If you sacrifice something valuable or important, you give it up.

e.g. *sacrificing the interests of a British company in favour of an American deal.*

forego   forfeit   give up

sad

(adjective) If you are sad, you feel unhappy.

e.g. *I hated it when I left and saw her looking sad.*

down in the dumps   gloomy   melancholy   miserable   mournful   pensive   unhappy

safe

(adjective) If you are safe, you are not in any danger.

e.g. *They will bring you to a safe place where you can spend the next two or three days.*

safe and sound   secure   unharmed   unhurt   unscathed

salvation

(noun) When someone's salvation takes place, they are saved from harm or evil.

e.g. *Burgoyne's troops were now beyond salvation.*

deliverance   escape   redemption   rescue   saving

satisfy

(verb) To satisfy someone means to give them enough of something to make them pleased or contented.

e.g. *compromises designed to satisfy everyone but failing to please anyone.*

answer appease assuage content gratify indulge

satisfying

(adjective) Something that is satisfying gives you a feeling of pleasure and fulfilment.

e.g. *the most satisfying moment of his whole career.*

enriching fulfilling gratifying pleasing rewarding satisfactory

savage

(adjective) cruel and violent.

e.g. *savage fighting.*

barbarous bloodthirsty brutal cruel ferocious murderous uncivilized vicious

save

(verb) If you save someone, you rescue them or help to keep them safe.

e.g. *He saved a whole family during the blitz.*

deliver free liberate redeem rescue

say

(verb) When you say something, you speak words.

e.g. *He phoned and said I'm not to ask you any questions.*

comment declare mention remark speak state utter

saying

(noun) A saying is a well-known sentence or phrase that tells you something about human life.

e.g. *Besides, there is a saying in England, is there not, "Why keep a dog and bark yourself?"*

adage aphorism axiom maxim motto proverb saw

scare

(verb) If something scares you, it frightens you.

e.g. *"Is it a warning? Are they trying to scare us?" he wondered.*

alarm frighten shock startle terrify

scathing

(adjective) harsh and scornful.

e.g. *They were scathing about his job.*

caustic cutting sarcastic scornful virulent vitriolic withering

scatter

1. (verb) To scatter things means to throw or drop them all over an area.

e.g. *hobbling out to scatter scraps for the hens.*

fling litter shower sprinkle strew

2. If people scatter, they suddenly move away in different directions.

e.g. *like the end of a holiday when new acquaintances scatter at the airport.*

disband disperse

scold

(verb) If you scold someone, you tell them off.

e.g. *He never scolded or criticized them.*

admonish berate castigate chastise chide lecture rebuke reprimand reproach reprove tick off

scornful

(adjective) showing contempt.

e.g. *his scornful comment.*

contemptuous derisive disdainful mocking sardonic scathing slighting sneering supercilious

scream

(verb) If you scream, you shout or cry in a loud, high-pitched voice.

e.g. *A few of the crowd screamed and ran away.*

cry howl screech shriek yell

scrounge

(verb; an informal word) If you scrounge something, you get it by asking for it rather than by earning or buying it.

e.g. *a bag of oranges scrounged from the hotel.*

beg cadge sponge

scruffy

(adjective) dirty and untidy.

e.g. *four scruffy youths.*

disreputable seedy slovenly tatty unkempt

search

1. (verb) If you search for something, you look for it in several places.

e.g. *Suppose we search the house first?*

check comb examine hunt look for ransack scour seek sift through

2. (noun) A search is an attempt to find something.

e.g. *After a long search he found it.*

examination hunt inquiry investigation pursuit quest

secret

(adjective) Something that is secret is told to only a small number of people and hidden from everyone else.

e.g. *a secret meeting.*

clandestine classified confidential covert hush-hush underground

secretive

(adjective) Secretive people tend to hide their feelings and intentions.

e.g. *Jake was very secretive about his family affairs.*

close enigmatic furtive reticent stealthy surreptitious

section

(noun) A section of something is one of the parts it is divided into.

e.g. *The first section of the motorway was opened in 1975.*

instalment part portion segment

sediment

(noun) Sediment is solid material that settles at the bottom of a liquid.

e.g. *Let the sediment created by this fermentation settle.*

deposit dregs grounds lees residue

see

(verb) If you see something, you are looking at it or you notice it.

e.g. *I could see Jenny in the studio.*

catch sight of discern distinguish espy glimpse notice observe perceive sight spot spy

selection

(noun) A selection of things or people is a set of them chosen from a larger group.

e.g. *a short selection of my personal favourites.*

assortment collection medley miscellany range variety

selfish

(adjective) caring only about yourself, and not about other people.

e.g. *The ruling group placed selfish interests above those of mankind.*

egotistic greedy mercenary self-seeking ungenerous

self-righteous

(adjective) convinced that you are better or more virtuous than other people.

e.g. *derided on all sides as smug, self-righteous bores.*

complacent priggish sanctimonious self-satisfied smug superior

sell

(verb) If a shop sells something, it has it available for people to buy.

e.g. *a tobacconist that sells stamps.*

handle market retail stock trade in

send

(verb) If you send something to someone, you arrange for it to be delivered to them.

e.g. *Some manufacturers will send you a card to remind you.*

consign convey direct dispatch forward transmit

sensational

(adjective) causing great excitement and interest.

e.g. *the most sensational product of the U.S. movie industry.*

amazing astounding breathtaking dramatic melodramatic shocking spectacular thrilling

sensible

(adjective) showing good sense and judgment.

e.g. *We failed to develop a sensible policy for controlling the export of steel.*

balanced intelligent judicious level-headed logical politic practical pragmatic prudent rational realistic shrewd sound wise

sensual

(adjective) showing or suggesting a liking for sexual pleasures.

e.g. *She has a wide, sensual mouth.*

carnal erotic sensuous sultry voluptuous

sentimental

(adjective) feeling or expressing tenderness, romance, or sadness to an exaggerated extent.

e.g. *sentimental love stories.*

emotional maudlin mawkish nostalgic romantic sloppy soppy tender touching

separate

1. (verb) To separate people or things means to cause them to be apart from each other.

e.g. *taking steps to separate myself from religious bias and bigotry.*

alienate detach dissociate estrange segregate sever

2. If people or things separate, they move away from each other.

e.g. *In solution, electrovalent compounds separate into their constituent ions.*

break up diverge divide part part company split up

series

(noun) A series of things is a number of them coming one after the other.

e.g. *a series of loud explosions.*

chain run sequence string succession train

serious

1. (adjective) A serious problem or situation is very bad and worrying.

e.g. *I hope it turns out to be nothing serious.*

acute critical grave momentous pressing severe urgent weighty worrying

2. People who are serious are thoughtful, quiet, and slightly humourless.

e.g. *She has a serious, thoughtful face.*

earnest sedate sober solemn thoughtful

service

(verb) When a machine or vehicle is serviced, it is examined, adjusted, and cleaned so that it will continue working efficiently.

e.g. *She made a mental note to have the car serviced.*

overhaul recondition

servile

(adjective) too eager to obey people.

e.g. *respectful of rank to a servile degree.*

fawning grovelling ingratiating obsequious smarmy subservient sycophantic unctuous

set

1. (verb) If you set a time, price, or level, you decide what it will be.

e.g. *preconditions set by the prime minister.*

allocate arrange assign establish fix name schedule settle specify

2. (adjective) Something that is set is fixed and not varying.

e.g. *a set charge.*

agreed appointed arranged definite firm fixed hard and fast inflexible prescribed regular rigid settled

shabby

(adjective) old and worn in appearance.

e.g. *a shabby overcoat.*

faded frayed threadbare worn worn-out

shake

(verb) If something shakes, it moves from side to side or up and down with small, quick movements.

e.g. *The plane was shaking to an uncomfortable degree.*

judder quake quiver rock shiver shudder sway tremble vibrate

shameless

(adjective) behaving in an indecent or unacceptable way, but showing no shame or embarrassment.

e.g. *shameless dishonesty.*

audacious barefaced brash brazen flagrant unabashed wanton

shape

(noun) The shape of something is the form or pattern of its outline, for example whether it is round or square.

e.g. *his shape unrecognizable under layers of non-regulation clothing.*

configuration contours cut form outline

shapely

(adjective) A shapely woman has an attractive figure.

e.g. *an attractive, shapely lady.*

buxom curvaceous voluptuous

share

(noun) A share of something is a portion of it.

e.g. *He wanted a glutton's share of the takings.*

allocation allotment cut part portion quota ration

sharp

(adjective) A sharp person is quick to notice or understand things.

e.g. *You've got to be sharp to get ahead.*

acute alert astute bright clever keen knowing observant perceptive quick

shining

(adjective) Shining things are very bright, usually because they are reflecting light.

e.g. *shining stainless steel tables.*

bright brilliant gleaming glistening glowing incandescent phosphorescent shimmering sparkling

shock

1. (verb) If something shocks you, it upsets you because it is unpleasant and unexpected.

e.g. *I was shocked by his appearance.*

appal disquiet horrify shake stagger stun

2. You can say that something shocks you when it offends you because it is rude or immoral.

e.g. *She went out of her way to shock the more conventional officers.*

disgust outrage scandalize

short

(adjective) If you are short with someone, you speak to them crossly.

e.g. *Extreme fatigue made her short with him.*

abrupt brusque curt offhand sharp terse

shout

(verb) If you shout something, you say it very loudly.

e.g. *He shouted something to his brother.*

bawl bellow call cry roar scream yell

show

1. (verb) To show that something exists or is true means to prove it.

e.g. *The survey showed that 29 per cent would now approve the treaty.*

demonstrate indicate prove reveal teach

2. If a picture shows something, it represents it.

e.g. *The painting shows supporters and crowd scenes.*

depict exhibit reveal

3. If something shows a quality or characteristic, you can see that it has it.

e.g. *Her sketches and watercolours showed promise.*

demonstrate display reveal

4. If you show your feelings, you let people see them.

e.g. *Savage was flustered, but too proud to show it.*
disclose divulge reveal

5. (noun) A show of a feeling is behaviour in which you show it.
e.g. *a show of optimism.*
demonstration display

showy

(adjective) large or bright and intended to impress people.
e.g. *a showy house.*
flamboyant flashy garish gaudy loud ostentatious

shrewd

(adjective) Someone who is shrewd is intelligent and makes good judgements.
e.g. *He was really ahead of his time, a shrewd business man.*
acute astute canny discerning keen knowing perceptive perspicacious sharp

shy

(adjective) A shy person is nervous and uncomfortable in the company of other people.
e.g. *He was quiet, soft-spoken, a shy man.*
bashful diffident mousy retiring shrinking timid

sick

(adjective) If you feel sick, you feel as if you are going to vomit.
e.g. *feeling sick during the night.*
ill indisposed nauseated nauseous queasy squeamish

sign

1. (noun) A sign is a mark or symbol with a particular meaning.
e.g. *a minus sign.*
cipher device emblem figure logo mark symbol

2. A sign is also a gesture with a particular meaning.

e.g. *She communicated with the women by signs.*
cue gesticulation gesture indication signal

silence

(verb) To silence someone or something means to stop them talking or making a noise.
e.g. *There was laughter again, which the corporal silenced.*
cut off deaden gag hush muffle muzzle quell quieten stifle

silent

(adjective) If you are silent, you are not saying anything.
e.g. *She stood silent, listening.*
dumb hushed mum mute quiet soundless speechless

silly

(adjective) foolish or childish.
e.g. *It was silly to make a fuss over seating arrangements.*
absurd asinine childish daft fatuous foolish pointless puerile ridiculous senseless stupid witless

similarity

(noun) If there is a similarity between things, they are similar in some way.
e.g. *There was no similarity between it and the writing in the ransom note.*
affinity closeness correspondence likeness relation resemblance

sin

1. (noun) Sin is wicked and immoral behaviour.
e.g. *a snare and delusion leading towards sin.*
evil iniquity transgression wickedness wrong

2. (verb) To sin means to do something wicked and immoral.
e.g. *They had sinned by omission.*
err lapse transgress

sincere

(adjective) If you are sincere, you say things that you really mean.

e.g. *a sincere expression of friendliness.*

genuine guileless heartfelt honest true

situation

(noun) A situation is what is happening in a particular place at a particular time.

e.g. *the political situation.*

case circumstances condition position state of affairs

size

(noun) The size of something is how big or small it is.

e.g. *the size of the audience.*

dimensions magnitude measurement proportions

skilful

(adjective) If you are skilful at something, you can do it very well.

e.g. *There are singers and skilful musicians.*

able adept adroit consummate deft dexterous expert handy masterly practised professional proficient skilled

skill

(noun) Skill is the knowledge and ability that enables you to do something well.

e.g. *her skill as an actress.*

ability art artistry craft dexterity expertise finesse knack proficiency prowess talent

skimp

(verb) If you skimp on a task, you do it carelessly or using less material than you should.

e.g. *Don't skimp on fabric or you'll spoil the draping effect.*

scrimp stint

slander

(noun) Slander is something untrue and malicious said about someone.

e.g. *the spreading of evil gossip and slander.*

calumny misrepresentation slur smear vilification

slaughter

(noun) Slaughter is the killing of many people.

e.g. *joining in an orgy of slaughter and pillage.*

bloodshed carnage extermination killing massacre murder slaying

sleep

(noun) If you have a sleep, you sleep for a while.

e.g. *He'll be ready for a sleep soon.*

doze forty winks *informal* kip *British slang* nap slumber snooze *informal*

sleepy

(adjective) tired and ready to go to sleep.

e.g. *I slept right through until six, and I still feel sleepy.*

dozy drowsy lethargic sluggish somnolent

slender

(adjective) attractively thin and graceful.

e.g. *a slender girl with long hair.*

slim svelte willowy

slogan

(noun) A slogan is a short, easily-remembered phrase used in advertising or by a political party.

e.g. *badges with the slogan "A woman's right to work".*

catchphrase catchword jingle motto watchword

slope

1. (noun) A slope is a flat surface that is at an angle, so that one

end is higher than the other.

e.g. *down the grass slope leading to the river.*

incline slant tilt

2. The slope of something is the angle at which it slopes.

e.g. *a slope of ten degrees.*

gradient inclination

slow

(adjective) moving, happening, or doing something with very little speed.

e.g. *children moving in a slow circle around the room.*

creeping dawdling lagging lazy leaden leisurely loitering measured plodding ponderous sluggish unhurried

sly

(adjective) A sly person is cunning and good at deceiving people.

e.g. *She was pictured as a sly manipulator.*

artful crafty cunning devious scheming shifty sneaky underhand wily

small

1. (adjective) Small means not large in size, number, or amount.

e.g. *She began to pace round the small room.*

diminutive little miniature petite scanty slight

2. Small also means not important or significant.

e.g. *small changes.*

insignificant lesser limited minor modest negligible paltry petty trifling trivial

smell

(noun) The smell of something is a quality it has which you perceive through your nose.

e.g. *a smell of damp wood.*

aroma odour perfume scent whiff

smooth

1. (adjective) A smooth surface has no roughness in it.

e.g. *The boulders were smooth and slippery.*

even flat flush glassy horizontal level plain sleek unbroken unwrinkled

2. If you say that a man is smooth, you mean that he is smart, confident, and polite in a way you find rather unpleasant.

e.g. *A very smooth fellow, he seemed to know everything that was going on.*

debonair facile glib slick suave urbane

snub

(noun) A snub is an insulting remark or a piece of rude behaviour.

e.g. *a deliberate snub to them.*

affront insult rebuff rejection slight

soak

(verb) When a liquid soaks something, it makes it very wet.

e.g. *his khaki shirt soaked with sweat.*

bathe drench immerse saturate steep

sociable

(adjective) Sociable people are friendly and enjoy talking to other people.

e.g. *Usually so outgoing and sociable, she'd grown withdrawn.*

companionable convivial cordial friendly gregarious outgoing

society

(noun) Society is the people in a particular country or region.

e.g. *a major problem in society.*

civilization community culture general public people

soil

(noun) Soil is the top layer on the surface of the earth in which

plants grow.
e.g. *Crops failed on this poor, sandy soil.*
earth ground land

solitude

(noun) Solitude is the state of being alone.
e.g. *She enjoyed her moments of solitude before the pressures of the day began.*
isolation loneliness privacy retirement seclusion

solve

(verb) If you solve a problem or a question, you find a solution or answer to it.
e.g. *It seemed an easy problem to solve.*
answer clear up crack decipher get to the bottom of resolve unravel work out

sophisticated

(adjective) Sophisticated people have refined or cultured tastes or habits.
e.g. *He was sophisticated and amusing, an attentive escort.*
cosmopolitan cultivated cultured suave urbane worldly

sordid

(adjective) dirty, unpleasant, or depressing.
e.g. *the sordid guest house.*
seedy sleazy squalid wretched

sore

(adjective) If part of your body is sore, it causes you pain and discomfort.
e.g. *His hand was sore and swollen.*
inflamed painful raw sensitive smarting tender

sorry

(adjective) If you are sorry about something, you feel sadness, regret, or sympathy because of it.

e.g. *I was so sorry to hear about your husband.*

apologetic contrite distressed penitent regretful remorseful repentant shamefaced

sort

(noun) The different sorts of something are the different types of it.

e.g. *five different sorts of biscuits.*

brand category class denomination form ilk kind make quality species style type variety

spacious

(adjective) having or providing a lot of space.

e.g. *the spacious living room.*

capacious commodious expansive extensive roomy sizable

spare

(adjective) extra to what is needed.

e.g. *I have lots of spare time.*

additional emergency extra free reserve superfluous surplus unoccupied unused

sparkle

(verb) If something sparkles, it shines with a lot of small, bright points of light.

e.g. *Long diamond earrings sparkled at her neck.*

flash gleam glint glisten glitter scintillate twinkle

speak

(verb) When you speak, you use your voice to say words.

e.g. *She started to speak, and then stopped.*

converse discourse talk utter

specific

1. (adjective) Something that is specific to a thing is connected with that thing only.

e.g. *specific areas of difficulty.*

especial particular peculiar special

2. precise and exact.

e.g. *She will ask for specific answers.*

certain definite exact explicit precise unequivocal

spectacular

(adjective) Something spectacular is very impressive or dramatic.

e.g. *spectacular views of Snowdonia.*

breathtaking daring dazzling dramatic magnificent sensational stunning

spectator

(noun) A spectator is a person who is watching something.

e.g. *The team was allowed to depart to the cheers of the spectators.*

bystander eyewitness observer onlooker viewer watcher witness

speech

(noun) A speech is a formal talk given to an audience.

e.g. *the opportunity to make his usual conventional little speech.*

address discourse lecture oration talk

speed

1. (noun) The speed of something is the rate at which it moves, travels, or happens.

e.g. *The speed can be modified.*

pace rate tempo velocity

2. Speed is very fast movement or travel.

e.g. *The balloon dropped earthwards with considerable speed.*

alacrity haste rapidity swiftness

spiteful

(adjective) A spiteful person does or says nasty things to people deliberately to hurt them.

e.g. *saying spiteful things about them behind their backs.*

bitchy catty malevolent malicious mean nasty vicious vindictive

splendid

(adjective) beautiful and impressive.

e.g. *a splendid Victorian mansion.*

glorious grand impressive lavish luxurious magnificent sumptuous

split

1. (verb) If something splits or if you split it, it divides into two or more parts.

e.g. *Split the wages between you.*

cleave crack divide open part separate

2. (noun) A split between two things is a division or difference between them.

e.g. *the split between rugby league and rugby union.*

breach break cleft division estrangement rift rupture schism

spoil

1. (verb) If you spoil something, you prevent it from being successful or satisfactory.

e.g. *nothing to spoil the perfect day.*

damage destroy mar ruin scupper *informal* undo wreck

2. To spoil children means to give them everything they want, with harmful effects on their character.

e.g. *Elizabeth was the one she did spoil.*

coddle cosset indulge mollycoddle pamper pet

spotless

(adjective) perfectly clean.

e.g. *a spotless starched white overall.*

immaculate impeccable pristine pure

stage

(noun) A stage is a part of a process that lasts for a period of time.

e.g. *the last stage of your studies here with us.*

juncture period phase point

stagger

(verb) If you stagger, you walk unsteadily because you are ill or drunk.

e.g. *Caught off balance, he staggered back a pace.*

lurch reel sway totter

stale

(adjective) Stale food or air is no longer fresh.

e.g. *a stale smoky atmosphere.*

decayed dry faded fetid flat fusty musty old sour

stare

(verb) If you stare at something, you look at it for a long time.

e.g. *He turned his head to stare at her.*

gape gawk gaze goggle look watch

start

1. (verb) If something or someone starts, or you start something, the first action or the first part of something happens.

e.g. *She started a programme of aerobic dancing.*

begin commence embark upon initiate instigate originate set up

2. (noun) The start of something is the point or time at which it begins.

e.g. *at the start of the campaign.*

beginning birth commencement foundation inauguration

inception opening outset

stationary

(adjective) not moving.

e.g. *a stationary car.*

immobile inert motionless standing static

status

(noun) A person's status is their position and importance in society.

e.g. *their newly acquired status in the community.*

position prestige rank rating standing

stay

(verb) If you stay in a place, you do not move away from it.

e.g. *She stayed in bed until noon.*

continue linger remain stop tarry wait

steady

1. (adjective) Something that is steady develops gradually without interruptions.

e.g. *a steady rise in prices.*

consistent constant continuous incessant nonstop persistent regular unbroken uninterrupted

2. firm and not shaking or wobbling.

e.g. *O'Brien held out a steady hand.*

firm fixed secure stable sure

steal

(verb) To steal something means to take it without permission and without intending to return it.

e.g. *I saw her steal an item of clothing.*

filch misappropriate nick *informal* pilfer pinch *informal* purloin thieve

steep

(adjective) A steep slope rises sharply and is difficult to go up.
e.g. *overlooking a steep descent to the river.*
precipitous sheer

steer

(verb) To steer a vehicle or boat means to control it so that it goes in the right direction.
e.g. *Milton steered erratically with his left hand.*
control direct guide pilot

sterile

(adjective) Sterile means completely clean and free from germs.
e.g. *She held a sterile pad pressed against the wound.*
antiseptic aseptic disinfected sterilized

stilted

(adjective) formal, unnatural, and rather awkward.
e.g. *a stilted conversation about American comics.*
artificial forced laboured stiff unnatural wooden

stimulate

(verb) To stimulate something means to encourage it to begin or develop.
e.g. *The purpose of this campaign is to stimulate discussion.*
animate arouse encourage enliven excite inspire kindle prompt provoke rouse whet

sting

(verb) If a part of your body stings, you feel a sharp tingling pain there.
e.g. *My leg began to sting painfully.*
hurt nip smart tingle

stink

(noun) A stink is a very unpleasant smell.

e.g. *a foul stink of burning rubber.*
pong *informal* reek stench

stomach

(noun) Your stomach is the organ inside your body where food is digested.
e.g. *His stomach felt hollow with excitement.*
abdomen belly gut tummy

stop

1. (verb) If you stop doing something, you no longer do it.
e.g. *We all stopped talking.*
cease desist discontinue finish leave off quit

2. To stop something means to prevent it.
e.g. *Did any of them try to stop you coming?*
bar block check frustrate hinder impede prevent restrain

store

(noun) A store of something is a supply kept for future use.
e.g. *collecting a huge store of facts.*
accumulation cache fund hoard reserve reservoir stock stockpile supply

story

(noun) A story is a description of imaginary people and events written or told to entertain people.
e.g. *The first story is about a soldier returning from service.*
account anecdote narrative saga tale yarn

strain

1. (verb) To strain something means to force it or use it more than is reasonable or normal.
e.g. *These increases have strained the resources of the smaller countries.*
extend overexert overtax overwork stretch tax

2. To strain food means to pour away the liquid from it.
e.g. *Strain any excess liquid into a separate container.*
filter sieve sift

3. (noun) Strain is worry and nervous tension.
e.g. *Overcrowding imposes severe mental strain.*
anxiety pressure stress tension

strange

1. (adjective) unusual or unexpected.
e.g. *Evie always wore such strange clothes.*
abnormal bizarre curious extraordinary fantastic freakish funny odd peculiar queer singular uncanny weird zany

2. not known, seen, or experienced before.
e.g. *She was alone in a strange country.*
alien exotic foreign new unfamiliar unknown

strength

1. (noun) Your strength is your physical energy and the power of your muscles.
e.g. *He was at the end of his strength.*
might robustness stamina toughness

2. You can refer to power or influence as strength.
e.g. *The campaign against pit closures gathered strength.*
energy force intensity muscle vigour

strengthen

(verb) To strengthen something means to give it more power, influence, or support and make it more likely to succeed.
e.g. *The attacks only served to strengthen their resolve.*
bolster brace consolidate fortify intensify reinforce stiffen support toughen

stress

1. (noun) Stress is worry and nervous tension.
e.g. *Regular exercise helps combat stress.*

anxiety pressure strain tension

2. (verb) If you stress a point, you emphasize it and draw attention to its importance.
e.g. *He had, he stressed, been forced to attack.*
accentuate emphasize highlight underline

3. (noun) Stress is emphasis put on a word or part of a word when it is pronounced, making it slightly louder.
e.g. *the importance of stress and intonation.*
accent emphasis

strict

1. (adjective) Someone who is strict controls other people very firmly.
e.g. *He felt that my uncle was too strict, too demanding.*
authoritarian firm rigorous severe stern

2. A strict rule must always be obeyed absolutely.
e.g. *strict instructions not to return before dinner.*
rigid stringent

stroll

1. (verb) To stroll means to walk slowly in a relaxed way.
e.g. *He rose and strolled nonchalantly towards the door.*
amble promenade saunter walk wander

2. (noun) A stroll is a slow, pleasurable walk.
e.g. *She would have liked to go for a stroll.*
airing constitutional ramble turn

strong

1. (adjective) Someone who is strong has powerful muscles.
e.g. *She was small and frail looking, but deceptively strong.*
brawny mighty muscular powerful stalwart stout strapping tough

2. Strong also means great in degree or intensity.
e.g. *a strong sense of responsibility.*
acute extreme fierce intense keen marked violent

structure

(noun) The structure of something is the way it is made, built, or organized.

e.g. *the structure of American society.*

arrangement composition constitution construction form formation make-up organization

strut

(verb) To strut means to walk in a stiff, proud way with your chest out and your head high.

e.g. *a truculent little man, who strutted around the deck shouting at us.*

parade prance swagger

stubborn

(adjective) Someone who is stubborn is determined not to change their opinion or course of action.

e.g. *an air of stubborn determination.*

dogged inflexible intransigent obdurate obstinate persistent pig-headed refractory wilful

stuffy

(adjective) If it is stuffy in a room, there is not enough fresh air.

e.g. *The room was stuffy but clean.*

airless close fusty heavy muggy oppressive stale stifling sultry

stupid

(adjective) showing lack of good judgment or intelligence and not at all sensible.

e.g. *The whole thing had been stupid and unnecessary.*

dense *informal* dim dull dumb *informal* indiscreet naive obtuse senseless simple slow slow-witted thick *informal*

style

(noun) A person or place that has style is smart, elegant, and fashionable.

e.g. *She had enormous talent and style, but had had no formal training.*

chic dash elegance flair panache refinement smartness sophistication stylishness

stylish

(adjective) smart, elegant, and fashionable.

e.g. *He wore a stylish, European-cut suit.*

chic dapper fashionable polished smart urbane

subdue

(verb) If soldiers subdue a group of people, they bring them under control by using force.

e.g. *It would be quite impossible to subdue the whole continent.*

control overcome overpower quell repress suppress

substance

(noun) Anything which is a solid, a powder, a liquid, or a paste can be referred to as a substance.

e.g. *a plate of some glutinous substance that she supposed was dessert.*

fabric material matter stuff

substitute

1. (verb) To substitute one thing for another means to use it instead of the other thing or to put it in the other thing's place.

e.g. *You can also make muffins by substituting syrup for the oil.*

exchange replace switch

2. (noun) If one thing is a substitute for another, it is used instead of it or put in its place.

e.g. *an acceptable substitute for the real thing.*

deputy equivalent replacement reserve stand-by stand-in stopgap surrogate

succeed

(verb) To succeed means to achieve the result you intend.

e.g. *She had the will to succeed.*

do well flourish manage prosper thrive triumph

suffice

(verb; a formal word) If something suffices, it is enough or adequate for a purpose.

e.g. *Half an hour should suffice.*

be sufficient do serve

suggest

1. (verb) If you suggest a plan or idea to someone, you mention it as a possibility for them to consider.

e.g. *I suggested she phone the hospital.*

advise advocate move propose recommend

2. If something suggests a particular thought or impression, it makes you think in that way or gives you that impression.

e.g. *Nothing you say suggests he is mentally ill.*

imply indicate

suggestion

(noun) A suggestion is a plan or idea that is mentioned as a possibility for someone to consider.

e.g. *He agreed readily to his father's suggestion.*

motion plan proposal proposition recommendation

suggestive

(adjective) Suggestive remarks or gestures make people think about sex.

e.g. *a suggestive leer.*

indecent indelicate naughty provocative racy ribald risqué rude saucy smutty titillating

suitable

(adjective) right or acceptable for a particular purpose or occasion.

e.g. *trying to think of a suitable reply.*

apposite appropriate apt due fit fitting opportune

proper right satisfactory

summary

(noun) A summary of something is a short account of its main points.

e.g. *a summary of the information contained in the charts.*

abstract outline précis recapitulation résumé review rundown synopsis

supervise

(verb) To supervise someone means to check and direct what they are doing to make sure that they do it correctly.

e.g. *appointed to supervise the household staff.*

control look after oversee preside superintend

supplement

(verb) To supplement something means to add something to it to improve it.

e.g. *Many village men supplemented their wages by fishing for salmon.*

augment boost complement top up

suppress

(verb) If an army or government suppresses an activity, it prevents people from doing it.

e.g. *suppressed by a massive show of military force.*

check curb quash quell repress stamp out

supreme

(adjective) Supreme is used to emphasize the greatness of something.

e.g. *the supreme achievement of the human race.*

chief crowning foremost paramount prime principal superlative ultimate

surpass

(verb; a formal word) To surpass someone or something means

to be better than them.

e.g. *Her recital that day surpassed all her previous performances.*

eclipse exceed excel outclass outdo outshine outstrip transcend

surplus

(noun) If there is a surplus of something there is more of it than is needed.

e.g. *A labour surplus existed in backward countries.*

excess glut overabundance plethora superfluity surfeit

surprised

(adjective) You feel surprised when something unexpected happens.

e.g. *She took it all in her stride without appearing the least surprised or pleased.*

amazed astonished disconcerted incredulous nonplussed startled taken aback

surrender

1. (verb) To surrender means to stop fighting and agree that the other side has won.

e.g. *Neither side is prepared to surrender.*

cede concede quit yield

2. (noun) Surrender is a situation in which one side in a fight agrees that the other side has won and gives in.

e.g. *They would, inexorably, be starved into surrender.*

capitulation submission

3. (verb) If you surrender to a temptation or feeling, you let it take control of you.

e.g. *It was easy to surrender to the charm of the place, to bask in the rosy glow of the past.*

capitulate give in submit succumb yield

4. To surrender something means to give it up to someone else.

e.g. *The gallery director surrendered his keys to the building manager.*

forego forfeit give up relinquish resign

surround

(verb) To surround someone or something means to be situated all around them.

e.g. *the stone wall which surrounded the pool.*

circle encircle enclose encompass envelop ring

surroundings

(plural noun) You can refer to the area and environment around a place or person as their surroundings.

e.g. *very comfortable surroundings.*

background element environment habitat milieu neighbourhood

survey

(verb) To survey something means to look carefully at the whole of it.

e.g. *The Duchess surveyed the room critically.*

appraise assess examine inspect look over review scan study view

suspicion

(noun) Suspicion is the feeling of not trusting someone or the feeling that something is wrong.

e.g. *their politely worded but obvious suspicion of his story.*

distrust doubt mistrust scepticism wariness

suspicious

(adjective) Suspicious is used to describe things that make you think that there is something wrong with a situation.

e.g. *suspicious circumstances.*

doubtful dubious fishy *informal* irregular questionable shady suspect

swap

(verb) To swap one thing for another means to replace the first thing with the second.

e.g. *a pack of cigarettes which I swapped for some eggs.*

barter exchange interchange switch trade

swarm

(verb) If a place is swarming with people, there are a lot of people there.

e.g. *When I got there the place was swarming with police.*

abound bristle crawl seethe teem throng

sweet

(adjective) attractive and delightful.

e.g. *a sweet little baby.*

adorable appealing beautiful charming cute engaging winning winsome

swerve

(verb) To swerve means to suddenly change direction to avoid colliding with something.

e.g. *Twice he had to swerve violently to avoid potholes.*

deviate diverge sheer swing veer

swollen

(adjective) Something that is swollen has swelled up.

e.g. *The flesh above the wound was swollen and discoloured.*

bloated distended enlarged inflamed puffy

symbol

(noun) A symbol is a shape, design, or idea that is used to represent something.

e.g. *The fish has long been a symbol of Christianity.*

emblem logo representation sign token

symbolic

(adjective) Something that is symbolic has a special meaning that is considered to represent something else.

e.g. *The card is symbolic of new beginnings.*

allegorical emblematic figurative metaphorical representative

sympathy

(noun) Sympathy is kindness and understanding towards someone who is in difficulties.

e.g. *His face was cold, without sympathy.*

commiseration compassion condolence pity tenderness understanding

system

(noun) A system is an organized way of doing or arranging something according to a fixed plan or set of rules.

e.g. *an effective system of information gathering.*

method organization procedure process routine scheme structure

T t

tackle

(verb) If you tackle a difficult task, you start dealing with it in a determined way.

e.g. *The daughters had to tackle the household washing.*

apply yourself to   begin   deal with   get to grips with   set about   take on   undertake

tact

(noun) Tact is the ability to see when a situation is difficult or delicate and to handle it without upsetting or offending people.

e.g. *She had made her point with the utmost tact.*

consideration   delicacy   diplomacy   discretion   sensitivity   thoughtfulness

talent

(noun) Talent is the natural ability to do something well.

e.g. *my talent for debate.*

ability   aptitude   bent   capacity   flair   genius   gift   knack

talk

1. (verb) When you talk, you say things to someone.

e.g. *As they passed I heard them talking.*

chat   chatter   converse   gossip   natter *informal*   peak

2. (noun) Talk is discussion or gossip.

e.g. *When the others were there, the talk was often political.*

chat   conversation   gossip

3. A talk is an informal speech.

e.g. *long and interesting talks on farming and cattle raising.*

address   discourse   lecture   oration   speech

talkative

(adjective) talking a lot.

e.g. *a talkative bore.*

chatty garrulous long-winded loquacious verbose voluble wordy

task

(noun) A task is any piece of work which has to be done.

e.g. *the huge task of cleaning up.*

assignment chore duty enterprise exercise job labour mission undertaking work

taste

1. (verb) If food or drink tastes of something, it has that flavour.

e.g. *a red meat that tastes like beef.*

savour smack

2. (noun) If you have a taste for something, you enjoy it.

e.g. *a taste for publicity.*

appetite desire fancy fondness inclination liking partiality penchant relish

tax

(noun) Tax is an amount of money that citizens have to pay to the government so that it can provide public services such as health care and education.

e.g. *I pay tax on my wages.*

duty excise levy rate tariff toll

teach

1. (verb) If you teach someone something, you give them instructions so that they know about it or know how to do it.

e.g. *They can teach children to read.*

coach drill educate instruct school show train tutor

2. If you teach someone to think or behave in a certain way, you persuade them to think or behave in that way.

e.g. *She had been taught to be tough.*

direct educate instruct school train tutor

team

(noun) Any group of people who work together can be called a team.

e.g. *a team of gardeners.*

band body bunch company crew gang group set squad

tear

(noun) A tear in something is a hole that has been made in it.

e.g. *a tear in the muscle above the knee.*

hole laceration rip rupture

tell

(verb) If you tell someone something, you let them know about it.

e.g. *I told him what had happened.*

announce communicate express inform narrate notify proclaim recount relate reveal say speak state utter

temperance

(noun) Temperance is the habit of not drinking alcohol.

e.g. *a lifetime of labour and strict temperance.*

abstemiousness abstinence

tempt

(verb) If you tempt someone, you try to persuade them to do something by offering them something they want.

e.g. *Bargain prices tempt the shopper.*

attract draw entice invite lead on lure

tend

(verb) If something tends to happen, it happens usually or often.

e.g. *My mind tends to wander.*

be disposed to be liable to be prone to gravitate incline lean lean towards

tendency

(noun) A tendency is a habit, trend, or type of behaviour that happens very often.

e.g. *a tendency to be critical.*

bias disposition inclination leaning liability penchant predilection predisposition proclivity propensity

tender

(adjective) Someone who is tender has gentle and caring feelings.

e.g. *He was kindly and tender.*

affectionate caring compassionate gentle humane kind loving sensitive sympathetic warm

tense

(adjective) If you are tense, you are worried and nervous and cannot relax.

e.g. *Do you feel tense or anxious for no good reason?*

edgy jumpy keyed up nervous overwrought restless strained uptight wired

texture

(noun) The texture of something is the way it feels when you touch it.

e.g. *a smooth texture.*

consistency feel grain weave

theft

(noun) Theft is the crime of stealing.

e.g. *non-violent crimes such as theft and burglary.*

larceny pilfering robbery stealing thieving

theory

(noun) A theory is an idea or set of ideas that is meant to explain something.

e.g. *Darwin's theory of evolution.*

e.g. *Darwin's theory of evolution.*

assumption conjecture guess hypothesis speculation

thin

(adjective) A thin person or animal has very little fat on their body.

e.g. *She was thin as a wishbone.*

bony lank lanky lean meagre scraggy scrawny skinny slender slight slim spare spindly

thing

(noun) A thing is an object, rather than a plant, an animal, a human being, or something abstract.

e.g. *I threw a few things into a bag.*

article item object

think

1. (verb) When you think about ideas or problems, you use your mind to consider them.

e.g. *Dad was thinking about going home.*

brood cogitate consider contemplate deliberate meditate mull over muse ponder reason reflect ruminate

2. If you think something, you have the opinion that it is true or the case.

e.g. *I think she has a secret boyfriend.*

believe consider deem feel guess *chiefly U.S.* hold imagine judge presume reckon suppose surmise

thought

(noun) Thought is the activity of thinking.

e.g. *She was lost in thought.*

cogitation consideration contemplation deliberation meditation musing reflection rumination thinking

thoughtful

1. (adjective) When someone is thoughtful, they are quiet and serious because they are thinking about something.

e.g. *Dennis was thoughtful, saying very little.*
contemplative meditative musing pensive reflective

2. A thoughtful person remembers what other people want or need, and tries to be kind to them.
e.g. *People aren't always as thoughtful as we would like them to be.*
attentive caring considerate helpful kind kindly solicitous

threaten

(verb) If someone or something threatens a person or thing, they are likely to harm them.
e.g. *the disease that threatens him.*
endanger jeopardize menace

thrill

(noun) A thrill is a sudden feeling of great excitement, pleasure, or fear; also any event or experience that gives you such a feeling.
e.g. *the thrill of revenge.*
buzz *slang* charge *slang* kick *informal*

throw

(verb) When you throw something you are holding, you move your hand quickly and let it go, so that it moves through the air.
e.g. *He threw away the bottle.*
bowl cast catapult chuck fling heave hurl pitch send shy sling toss

tidy

1. (adjective) Something that is tidy is neat and arranged in an orderly way.
e.g. *Ian's room was tidy.*
methodical neat ordered orderly shipshape spick and span spruce trim uncluttered well-ordered

2. (verb) To tidy a place means to make it neat by putting things in their proper place.

e.g. *Brenda tidied and swept the house for me.*
clear neaten order put in order spruce up straighten

tie

(verb) If you tie one thing to another or tie it in a particular position, you fasten it using cord of some kind.
e.g. *Ropes were tied across each staircase.*
attach bind connect fasten join lash rope

tight

(adjective) stretched or pulled so as not to be slack.
e.g. *a tight cord.*
rigid stiff taut tense

tilt

(verb) If you tilt an object or it tilts, it changes position so that one end or side is higher than the other.
e.g. *She tilted her face to look up at me.*
cant heel incline lean list pitch slant slope tip

time

(noun) Time is what is measured in hours, days, and years.
e.g. *We have enough time to prepare ourselves well.*
interval period phase space span spell stretch term

timely

(adjective) happening at just the right time.
e.g. *Mr Tabor made a timely appearance.*
convenient opportune punctual well-timed

timid

(adjective) shy and having no courage or self-confidence.
e.g. *children who are timid and unsure of themselves.*
afraid bashful cowardly diffident faint-hearted fearful nervous pusillanimous retiring shy timorous

tiny

(adjective) extremely small.

e.g. *Scalpay is a tiny island.*

diminutive infinitesimal Lilliputian little miniature minuscule minute slight small wee

tire

1. (verb) If something tires you, it makes you use a lot of energy so that you want to rest or sleep.

e.g. *Hard work tired him easily.*

drain exhaust fatigue wear out weary

2. If you tire of something, you become bored with it.

e.g. *Children tire of chocolate eggs.*

weary

together

1. (adverb) If people do something together, they do it with each other.

e.g. *We all knew each other well and worked together.*

collectively en masse in unison jointly

2. If two things happen together, they happen at the same time.

e.g. *All B vitamins should be taken together.*

concurrently continuously simultaneously

tolerable

1. (adjective) able to be borne or put up with.

e.g. *The dreary music is barely tolerable.*

acceptable bearable endurable

2. fairly satisfactory or reasonable.

e.g. *a tolerable salary.*

acceptable adequate average fair middling okay *informal*

tolerate

1. (verb) If you tolerate things that you do not approve of or agree with, you allow them.

e.g. *They could no longer tolerate the way he runs the club.*

abide accept allow bear brook condone permit put up with sanction stand stick

2. If you can tolerate something, you accept it, even though it is unsatisfactory or unpleasant.

e.g. *He cannot tolerate losing.*

abide accept bear endure put up with stand stick stomach suffer swallow take

tomb

(noun) A tomb is a large grave for one or more corpses.

e.g. *the ornate tomb of the Charpentier family.*

crypt grave mausoleum sepulchre vault

tonic

(noun) You can refer to anything that makes you feel stronger or more cheerful as a tonic.

e.g. *It was a tonic just being with her.*

boost pick-me-up stimulant

tool

(noun) A tool is any hand-held instrument or piece of equipment that you use to help you do a particular kind of work.

e.g. *a cutting tool.*

appliance contrivance device gadget implement instrument machine utensil

top

1. (noun) The top of something is its highest point, part, or surface.

e.g. *the top of the mountain.*

apex crest crown head height peak pinnacle summit vertex zenith

2. The top of a bottle, jar, or tube is its cap or lid.

e.g. *a milk bottle top.*

cap cover lid stopper

torment

(noun) A torment is something that causes extreme pain and unhappiness.

e.g. *It's a torment to see them staring at me.*

bane blight plague scourge torture

toss

(verb) If you toss something somewhere, you throw it there lightly and carelessly.

e.g. *The crowds tossed garlands at his feet.*

cast chuck *informal* fling lob pitch sling throw

total

(noun) A total is the number you get when you add several numbers together.

e.g. *Last year Blackpool had a total of 17 million tourists.*

aggregate full amount sum totality whole

touching

(adjective) causing feelings of sadness and sympathy.

e.g. *a touching book.*

affecting moving piteous pitiful poignant sad stirring

tough

(adjective) A tough substance is difficult to break.

e.g. *tough plastic.*

durable firm hard resilient solid strong sturdy

trade

1. (noun) Trade is the activity of buying, selling, or exchanging goods or services between people, firms, or countries.

e.g. *opportunities for trade in Eastern Europe.*

barter business commerce dealing traffic transactions

2. (verb) When people, firms, or countries trade, they buy, sell,

or exchange goods or services.
e.g. *goods from countries we trade with.*
bargain barter deal do business peddle traffic transact

tradition

(noun) A tradition is a custom or belief that has existed for a long time without changing.
e.g. *the British tradition of taking tea.*
convention custom habit institution ritual unwritten law

traditional

(adjective) A traditional organization or institution is one in which older methods are used rather than modern ones.
e.g. *a traditional school.*
conservative conventional orthodox

transparent

(adjective) If an object or substance is transparent, you can see through it.
e.g. *transparent clothing.*
clear diaphanous filmy limpid see-through translucent

transport

(verb) When goods or people are transported from one place to another, they are moved there.
e.g. *the van they had used to transport furniture.*
bear bring carry convey ferry fetch haul move shuttle take transfer

trap

1. (verb) Someone who traps animals catches them using traps.
e.g. *There were more ways to trap a tiger than by shooting it.*
catch corner ensnare net snare take

2. If you trap someone, you trick them so that they do or say something which they did not want to.
e.g. *I trapped him into marriage.*

beguile deceive dupe fool trick

travel

(verb) To travel means to go from one place to another.

e.g. *Peter has travelled throughout the world.*

commute go journey move proceed progress voyage

treacherous

(adjective) A treacherous person is likely to betray you and cannot be trusted.

e.g. *a treacherous friend.*

deceitful disloyal faithless false perfidious traitorous unfaithful unreliable

trip

(noun) A trip is a journey made to a place.

e.g. *your first trip abroad.*

excursion expedition jaunt journey outing voyage

trouble

1. (noun) Troubles are difficulties or problems.

e.g. *Solve all your money troubles.*

bother difficulty dilemma hassle *informal* misfortune predicament problem woe worry

2. (verb) If something troubles you, it makes you feel worried or anxious.

e.g. *It still troubles me when I get jittery.*

agitate annoy bother disconcert disquiet distress disturb harass hassle *informal* perturb upset vex worry

3. If you trouble someone for something, you disturb them in order to ask them for it.

e.g. *I'm sorry to trouble you again.*

bother inconvenience put out

true

(adjective) A true story or statement is based on facts and is not made up.

e.g. *Allegations that had been made in the book were true.*

accurate actual authentic bona fide correct exact factual genuine honest precise real right veracious veritable

truth

(noun) The truth is the facts about something, rather than things that are imagined or made up.

e.g. *I know she was telling the truth.*

accuracy actuality fact genuineness legitimacy precision reality veracity verity

try

1. (verb) To try to do something means to make an effort to do it.

e.g. *I tried to get some photos.*

aim attempt bid endeavour essay have a go *informal* have a shot *informal* have a stab *informal* make an effort seek strive struggle

2. (noun) A try is an attempt to do something.

e.g. *It was her first try at authorship.*

attempt bid effort endeavour essay go *informal* shot *informal* stab *informal*

turn

(noun) If it is your turn to do something, you have the right, chance, or duty to do it.

e.g. *It is his turn to take the stage.*

chance fling go opportunity period round shot *informal* spell stint try

twist

1. (verb) When you twist something you turn one end of it in one direction while holding the other end or turning it in the opposite direction.

e.g. *Twist the hair around your finger.*

coil curl entwine screw swivel wind wring

2. When something twists or is twisted, it moves or bends into a strange shape.

e.g. *His face twisted in anger.*

contort distort screw up warp

typical

(adjective) showing the most usual characteristics or behaviour.

e.g. *He looked the typical vicar.*

average characteristic classic conventional normal orthodox representative standard stock usual

typify

(verb) If something typifies a situation or thing, it is characteristic of it or a typical example of it.

e.g. *The story of Ian and Katherine is one that typifies our times.*

characterize embody epitomize exemplify illustrate personify

U u

ugly

(adjective) very unattractive in appearance.

e.g. *an ugly Victorian church in red brick.*

hideous unattractive unsightly

unbearable

(adjective) Something unbearable is so unpleasant or upsetting that you feel you cannot stand it.

e.g. *The pain was unbearable.*

intolerable unacceptable unendurable

unbelievable

1. (adjective) extremely great or surprising.

e.g. *unbelievable courage.*

astonishing fantastic incredible staggering

2. so unlikely that you cannot believe it.

e.g. *I can understand why my story must have seemed unbelievable to you.*

impossible improbable preposterous unthinkable

uncouth

(adjective) bad-mannered and unpleasant.

e.g. *a coarse, uncouth type of person.*

boorish coarse loutish rough unrefined vulgar

undeniable

(adjective) certainly true.

e.g. *It is undeniable that babies show individual differences at birth.*

incontrovertible indisputable indubitable irrefutable obvious

undermine

(verb) To undermine an idea, feeling, or system means to make it less strong or secure.

e.g. *a campaign to undermine his authority.*

erode sabotage sap subvert weaken

understand

(verb) If you understand what someone says, you know what they mean.

e.g. *She could speak and understand Russian.*

appreciate comprehend fathom follow grasp know make out perceive take in

understandable

(adjective) If something is understandable, people think it is normal or natural.

e.g. *Her father's fears were understandable, but I was able to tell him they were groundless.*

acceptable comprehensible excusable justifiable natural reasonable

understanding

1. (noun) If you have an understanding of something, you have some knowledge about it.

e.g. *little understanding of children's needs.*

appreciation awareness comprehension discernment grasp insight knowledge perception perspicacity

2. (adjective) kind and sympathetic.

e.g. *Thank you for being so understanding.*

compassionate considerate kind patient perceptive responsive sensitive tolerant

unimportant

(adjective) having very little significance or importance.

e.g. *Let us know if you remember anything, however unimportant it may seem.*

inconsequential insignificant marginal minor negligible paltry petty slight trifling trivial worthless

uninhibited

(adjective) If you are uninhibited, you behave freely and naturally and show your true feelings.

e.g. *They made him laugh out loud with uninhibited delight.*

abandoned candid frank free informal instinctive natural open relaxed spontaneous

unkind

(adjective) unpleasant and rather cruel.

e.g. *It had been a thoughtless, unkind act, whatever the reason for it.*

malicious mean nasty spiteful uncharitable

unlucky

1. (adjective) Someone who is unlucky has bad luck.

e.g. *those who were unlucky enough to incur his enmity.*

hapless luckless unfortunate wretched

2. Something that is unlucky is thought to cause bad luck.

e.g. *Thirteen is supposed to be an unlucky number.*

cursed doomed ill-fated inauspicious ominous

unproductive

(adjective) not producing anything useful.

e.g. *The meadows beyond were clotted with weeds and unproductive.*

barren fruitless futile idle sterile unprofitable useless

untidy

(adjective) not neat or well arranged.

e.g. *a respectable-looking house with a wildly untidy garden.*

chaotic disorderly higgledy-piggledy *informal* jumbled muddled topsy-turvy unkempt

unusual

(adjective) Something that is unusual does not occur very often.

e.g. *a formidable adversary, a man of quite unusual powers.*

abnormal anomalous curious different extraordinary irregular rare remarkable singular strange surprising uncommon unexpected

unwilling

(adjective) If you are unwilling to do something, you do not want to do it.

e.g. *unable to sleep yet unwilling to leave her bed.*

averse disinclined indisposed loath reluctant

upkeep

(noun) The upkeep of something is the continual process and cost of keeping it in good condition.

e.g. *a significant contribution to the upkeep of the estate.*

keep maintenance running subsistence

uproar

(noun) If there is uproar or an uproar, there is a lot of shouting and noise, often because people are angry.

e.g. *Harriet's voice could be heard over all the uproar.*

babel clamour commotion din furore hubbub outcry pandemonium riot rumpus tumult

upset

1. (adjective) unhappy or disappointed because something unpleasant has happened.

e.g. *He was still upset about the accident.*

agitated disconcerted dismayed distressed disturbed hurt troubled worried

2. (verb) If someone upsets something such as a procedure, they cause things to go wrong.

e.g. *data that upset all previous calculations of the earth's age.*

change disorganize disturb spoil

3. If you upset something, you turn it over or spill it accidentally.

e.g. *I accidentally bumped into a table and upset a statuette.*
capsize knock over overturn spill tip over topple over

urge

1. (noun) If you have an urge to do something, you have a strong wish to do it.
e.g. *an urge to confess.*
compulsion desire fancy impulse itch longing wish yearning

2. (verb) If you urge someone to do something, you try hard to persuade them to do it.
e.g. *Ginny urged her to stay on after the funeral.*
encourage exhort goad incite press spur on

urgent

(adjective) needing to be dealt with as soon as possible.
e.g. *She drafted replies to the most urgent letters.*
compelling critical crucial immediate imperative pressing

use

1. (verb) If you use something, you do something with it in order to do a job or achieve something.
e.g. *May I use your phone?*
employ utilize

2. (noun) The use of something is the act of using it.
e.g. *the use of force.*
application employment exercise operation usage utilization

useful

(adjective) If something is useful, you can use it to do something or to help you in some way.
e.g. *Each play is preceded by a useful introduction.*
advantageous beneficial effective helpful practical profitable valuable worthwhile

usual

(adjective) happening, done, or used most often.

e.g. *His razor and his toothbrush are in their usual places.*

accustomed customary everyday expected familiar general habitual normal ordinary routine standard

V v

vague

(adjective) If something is vague, it is not expressed or explained clearly, or you cannot see or remember it clearly.

e.g. *vague statements.*

dim hazy indefinite indeterminate indistinct nebulous obscure shadowy uncertain unclear unspecified woolly

valuable

(adjective) Something that is valuable has great value.

e.g. *a valuable necklace.*

costly invaluable precious prized treasured valued

variety

(noun) A variety of things is a number of different kinds of them.

e.g. *a wide variety of readers.*

array assortment collection diversity medley miscellany mixture range

various

(adjective) Various means of several different types.

e.g. *trees of various sorts.*

assorted differing disparate diverse miscellaneous sundry varied

venture

(noun) A venture is something new which involves the risk of failure or of losing money.

e.g. *a successful venture in television films.*

endeavour enterprise project speculation undertaking

verdict

1. (noun) In a law court, a verdict is the decision which states whether a prisoner is guilty or not guilty.

e.g. *a verdict of not guilty.*

finding judgment sentence

2. If you give a verdict on something, you give your opinion after thinking about it.

e.g. *The critics may have hated the film, but the public verdict was favourable.*

conclusion decision judgment opinion

very

(adverb) Very is used before words to emphasize them.

e.g. *very bad dreams.*

exceedingly extremely highly particularly really remarkably terribly unusually wonderfully

victory

(noun) A victory is a success in a battle or competition.

e.g. *a crushing victory over her opponents.*

conquest mastery success triumph win

view

1. (noun) Your views are your personal opinions.

e.g. *He went to jail for his political views.*

attitude belief feeling impression opinion sentiment

2. A view is everything you can see from a particular place.

e.g. *Her flat looked out onto a superb view of London.*

aspect landscape outlook panorama prospect scene vista

viewpoint

(noun) Your viewpoint is your attitude towards something.

e.g. *The film looks at the world from a child's viewpoint.*

outlook perspective point of view position stance standpoint view

villain

(noun) A villain is someone who harms others or breaks the law.

e.g. *He had to tackle an armed villain single-handed.*

blackguard criminal knave miscreant reprobate rogue scoundrel wretch

virtue

1. (noun) Virtue is thinking and doing what is morally right and avoiding what is wrong.

e.g. *a priest of great virtue.*

goodness integrity morality probity rectitude

2. A virtue of something is an advantage.

e.g. *The plan has the virtue of simplicity.*

advantage asset attribute merit strength

virtuous

(adjective) behaving with or showing moral virtue.

e.g. *a noble and virtuous existence.*

blameless excellent exemplary good honest moral pure righteous upright worthy

vital

(adjective) necessary or very important.

e.g. *vital evidence.*

cardinal critical crucial decisive essential imperative indispensable key significant

vivacious

(adjective) A vivacious person is attractively lively and high-spirited.

e.g. *Laura was a vivacious, intelligent woman.*

animated ebullient effervescent exuberant lively sparkling spirited

vivid

(adjective) very bright in colour or clear in detail.

e.g. *vivid memories.*
clear descriptive distinct glowing graphic intense powerful strong

vulnerable

(adjective) weak and without protection.
e.g. *Its aim is to keep vulnerable young people off the streets.*
defenceless exposed susceptible unprotected weak

W w

wake

(verb) When you wake or when something wakes you, you become conscious again after being asleep.

e.g. *A good night's sleep is essential if we are to wake refreshed.*

arouse   awake   awaken   rouse   stir   waken   wake up

wander

(verb) If you wander in a place, you walk around in a casual way.

e.g. *Visitors are free to wander around the gardens.*

drift   meander   ramble   roam   rove   straggle   stray   stroll

war

1. (noun) A war is a period of fighting between countries or states when weapons are used and many people may be killed.

e.g. *The president was broadcasting within hours of the outbreak of war.*

battle   conflict   fighting   fray   warfare

2. (verb) When two countries war with each other, they are fighting a war against each other.

e.g. *They warred with each other for supremacy.*

battle   clash   combat   contend   fight   struggle   wage war

warn

(verb) If you warn someone about a possible problem or danger, you tell them about it in advance so that they are aware of it.

e.g. *I warned him what it would be like.*

alert   caution   forewarn   give notice   tip off

waste

1. (verb) If you waste time, money, or energy, you use too much of it on something that is not important or necessary.

e.g. *If only he wouldn't waste his money on crazy cars.*

dissipate exhaust fritter misuse squander

2. (noun) Waste is the use of more money or some other resource than is necessary.

e.g. *It's a waste of our time and energy.*

dissipation extravagance prodigality profligacy squandering wastage

wasteful

(adjective) extravagant or causing waste by using resources in a careless and inefficient way.

e.g. *a wasteful use of the planet's resources.*

extravagant improvident prodigal profligate ruinous spendthrift uneconomical

wave

1. (verb) If you wave something, you hold it up and move it from side to side.

e.g. *The doctor waved a piece of paper at him.*

brandish flourish flutter shake wag wield

2. (noun) A wave is a ridge of water on the surface of the sea.

e.g. *lines of white foam where the waves broke on the beach.*

billow breaker ripple roller swell

3. A wave of a feeling is a steady increase in it which spreads through you or through a group of people.

e.g. *a wave of panic.*

outbreak rush surge upsurge

way

1. (noun) A way of doing something is how it is done.

e.g. *different ways of cooking fish.*

fashion manner means method mode procedure process system

2. The way to a particular place is the route that you take to get there.

e.g. *The tourists often get lost on their way to their hotels.*

approach course direction path road route

weak

1. (adjective) not having much strength.

e.g. *weak from lack of sleep.*

debilitated exhausted faint feeble infirm puny spent wasted weedy

2. Someone who is weak is easily influenced by other people.

e.g. *incompetent and weak leadership.*

cowardly effete impotent indecisive irresolute pathetic shaky soft spineless

weaken

(verb) If something weakens you, it causes you to lose some of your physical strength and energy.

e.g. *Toxins in the environment weaken our immune systems.*

debilitate enervate sap tire undermine

wealth

(noun) Wealth is the large amount of money, property, or other valuable things which someone owns.

e.g. *the attainment of great wealth and property.*

affluence assets fortune means opulence prosperity resources riches substance wealthiness

wealthy

(adjective) having a large amount of money, property, or other valuable things.

e.g. *a wealthy sugar plantation owner.*

affluent comfortable moneyed opulent prosperous rich well-off well-to-do

weird

(adjective) strange or bizarre.

e.g. *a weird religious cult.*

bizarre eerie ghostly grotesque mysterious odd outlandish queer strange uncanny unearthly unnatural

whim

(noun) A whim is a sudden desire or fancy.

e.g. *He uses his money to indulge his every whim.*

caprice fancy humour impulse notion quirk urge vagary

whip

(verb) If you whip a person or animal, you hit them with a whip.

e.g. *I saw him whipping his team of mules.*

beat flay flog lash scourge thrash

wicked

(adjective) very bad.

e.g. *a wicked thing to do.*

amoral atrocious corrupt evil fiendish heinous iniquitous nefarious shameful sinful vicious vile

wide

(adjective) If there is a wide variety, range, or selection of something, there are many different kinds of it.

e.g. *a wide range of colours.*

ample broad catholic comprehensive extensive general vast wide-ranging

widespread

(adjective) existing or happening over a large area or to a great extent.

e.g. *the widespread use of chemicals.*

extensive general prevalent rampant rife sweeping universal wholesale

wilful

(adjective) Someone who is wilful is obstinate and determined to get their own way.

e.g. *a wilful child.*

headstrong obstinate perverse self-willed stubborn wayward

willing

(adjective) If you are willing to do something, you will do it if someone wants you to.

e.g. *They are willing to make concessions.*

agreeable content disposed eager game *informal* happy prepared ready

winner

(noun) The winner of a prize, race, or competition is the person or thing that wins it.

e.g. *the winner of the Grand National.*

champ champion conqueror first master victor

wise

(adjective) Someone who is wise can use their experience and knowledge to make sensible decisions and judgments.

e.g. *a very wise and intelligent young lady.*

discerning enlightened erudite informed intelligent judicious perceptive sagacious sage shrewd

wish

1. (noun) A wish is a desire for something.

e.g. *She had no wish to argue.*

desire hankering inclination longing urge

2. (verb) If you wish to do something, you want to do it.

e.g. *He did not wish to go.*

desire long need want

witchcraft

(noun) Witchcraft is the skill or art of using magic powers, especially evil ones.

e.g. *a study of witchcraft and magic in early Britain.*

black magic sorcery wizardry

wither

(verb) When something withers or withers away, it becomes weaker until it no longer exists.

e.g. *Farmers in the Midwest have watched their crops wither because of drought conditions.*

atrophy decay decline droop fade languish perish shrivel wane waste away wilt

witness

(noun) A witness is someone who has seen an event such as an accident and can describe what happened.

e.g. *I was a witness in a court case a couple of months ago.*

bystander eyewitness observer onlooker spectator

wonder

1. (noun) A wonder is something or someone that surprises or amazes people.

e.g. *the wonders of modern technology.*

marvel miracle phenomenon prodigy rarity sight spectacle

2. Wonder is a feeling of surprise or amazement.

e.g. *her look of wonder the first time it snowed.*

admiration astonishment awe bewilderment curiosity surprise

wonderful

(adjective) very impressive.

e.g. *Nature is a wonderful thing.*

amazing astounding extraordinary magnificent marvellous miraculous wondrous

wood

(noun) A wood is a large area of trees growing near each other.

e.g. *Follow the road until you reach a wood on your right.*

copse forest grove thicket woodland

work

1. (noun) Work is a job you are paid to do.

e.g. *I can't find work.*

business calling employment job line occupation profession trade

2. Work is things that have to be done.

e.g. *I've got loads of work to do.*

assignment chore drudgery duty job task

3. (verb) If someone works a machine, they control or operate it.

e.g. *Do you know how to work this video recorder?*

control direct drive handle manage manipulate move operate ply use

4. If something such as an idea or a system works, it is successful.

e.g. *The housing benefit system is not working.*

function go perform run

worried

(adjective) unhappy and anxious about a problem or about something unpleasant that might happen.

e.g. *I'm worried about how long he's taking to finish this job.*

anxious apprehensive bothered concerned distraught distressed perturbed troubled uneasy upset

worry

1. (verb) If you worry, you feel anxious, fearful, and uneasy about a problem or about something unpleasant that might happen.

e.g. *Don't worry, Andrew, you can do it.*

agonize fret

2. If something worries you, it causes you to feel uneasy or fearful.

e.g. *a puzzle which had worried her all her life.*

alarm bother concern distress disturb perturb torment trouble unsettle

3. (noun) Worry is a feeling of unhappiness and unease caused by a problem or by thinking of something unpleasant that might happen.

e.g. *a major source of worry.*

anxiety apprehension concern disquiet

worsen

(verb) If a situation worsens or if something worsens it, it becomes more difficult, unpleasant, or unacceptable.

e.g. *Oil pollution seems to be worsening.*

aggravate compound decline degenerate deteriorate exacerbate sink

worship

1. (verb) If you worship someone or something, you love them or admire them very much.

e.g. *I went on a trip to Hollywood and saw how they worship old cars over there.*

adore idolize revere venerate

2. (noun) Worship is the feeling of respect, love, or admiration you feel for something or someone.

e.g. *rock stars treated as objects of worship.*

adoration adulation devotion homage reverence veneration

wrestle

(verb) When you wrestle with a problem, you try to deal with it.

e.g. *For decades mathematicians have wrestled with this problem.*

battle fight grapple strive struggle

wrinkle

(noun) Wrinkles are lines in someone's skin, especially on the face, which form as they grow old.

e.g. *a new anti-wrinkle cream.*

crease fold furrow line

wrong

1. (adjective) not correct or truthful.

e.g. *the wrong answer.*

erroneous false inaccurate incorrect mistaken unsound untrue

2. not working properly or unsatisfactory.

e.g. *There was nothing wrong with his eyesight.*

amiss awry defective faulty

3. bad or immoral.

e.g. *It is wrong to steal.*

bad dishonest evil immoral sinful unfair unjust unlawful wicked wrongful

wry

(adjective) A wry expression shows that you find a situation slightly amusing because you know more about it than other people.

e.g. *She cast a wry glance in Mary Ann's direction.*

ironic mocking quizzical sarcastic sardonic

Y y

young

1. (adjective) A young person, animal, or plant has not lived very long and is not yet mature.
e.g. *You're too young to start smoking.*
immature   juvenile   youthful

2. (noun) The young of an animal are its babies.
e.g. *She was like a tigress defending her young.*
issue   offspring   progeny